he *Things To Do With Your Computer* series
as been prepared for Signet by dilithium Press,
renowned publisher of high-quality, easy-to-
nderstand, technically accurate computer
books. No matter what personal computer you
use, Signet dilithium has a book for you.

THINGS TO DO WITH YOUR TI-99/4A COMPUTER

THINGS TO DO WITH YOUR COMMODORE® 64™ COMPUTER

THINGS TO DO WITH YOUR COMMODORE® VIC 20™ COMPUTER

THINGS TO DO WITH YOUR TRS-80® MODEL 4 COMPUTER

THINGS TO DO WITH YOUR TRS-80® MODEL 100 COMPUTER

THINGS TO DO WITH YOUR APPLE® COMPUTER

THINGS TO DO WITH YOUR IBM® PERSONAL COMPUTER

THINGS TO DO WITH YOUR ATARI® COMPUTER

THINGS TO DO WITH YOUR TRS-80® COLOR COMPUTER

THINGS TO DO WITH YOUR OSBORNE® COMPUTER

DILITHIUM Books From SIGNET

THINGS TO DO WITH YOUR IBM® PERSONAL COMPUTER

by

Jerry Willis

Merl Miller

Nancy Morrice

TRADEMARK ACKNOWLEDGEMENTS

Apple, Apple Computer, Inc.; Apple IIe, Apple Computer, Inc.; ATARI, Atari, Inc.; ATARI 400, 800, 1200XL, Atari, Inc.; Aquaris, Mattel Electronics, Inc.; CalcStar, MicroPro International Corporation; CAT modems, Novation, Inc.; Cdex, Cdex Corporation; Centipede, Atari, Inc.; Commodore 64, Commodore Business Machines, Inc.; CompuServe, CompuServe, Inc.; Context MBA, Context Management Systems; CP/M, Digital Research; Creature Creator, DesignWare, Inc.; dBase II, Ashton Tate, Inc.; Deadline, Infocom, Inc.; DEFENDER, Williams Electronics, Inc.; Diablo 620, 630, 630 KSR, Xerox Corporation; DIALOG, DIALOG Information Services; Donkey Kong, Nintendo; Dow Jones News/Retrieval Service, Dow Jones & Company, Inc.; Dr. LOGO, Digital Research; Eagle PC, Eagle Computer Inc.; EasyWriter II, Information Unlimited Software, Inc.; Epson FX-80, Epson America, Inc.; Facemaker, Spinnaker Software Corp.; Family Roots, Quinsept, Inc.; Fast Eddie, Sirius Software; FriendlyWare, FriendlySoft, Inc.; FriendlyWare PC Arcade, FriendlySoft, Inc.; Grammatik, Aspen Software Company; Home

(The following page constitutes an extension of this copyright page)

Accountant, The, Continental Software; IBM PC, International Business Machines Corp.; IBM XT, International Business Machines Corp.; InfoStar, MicroPro International Corporation; Knowledge Index, DIALOG Information Services; LogiMate, LogiTech, Inc.; LogiMouse, LogiTech, Inc.; Lotus 1-2-3, Lotus Development Corporation; MasterType, Lightning Software; MailMerge, MicroPro International Corporation; PAC-MAN, Bally Midway Manufacturing Co.; PeachText, Peachtree Software, Inc.; SAT Exam Prep Series, Krell Software; Shelby Lyman Chess Tutorial, Krell Software; Smith-Corona TP-1, Smith-Corona, Inc.; Snooper Troops, Spinnaker Software Corporation; Source, The, Source Telecomputing; Spellicopter, DesignWare, Inc.; SpellStar, MicroPro International Corporation; Spyder, Mirror Images Software; StarIndex, MicroPro International Corporation; SuperCalc, Sorcium; Suspended, Infocom, Inc.; TRS-80 Model III, Tandy Corporation; TRS-80 Model 4, Tandy Corporation; UCSD Pascal, Regents of the University of California, San Diego; Vis/Bridge/DJ, Solution, Inc.; VisiCalc, VisiCorp; Viz-A-Con, Abacus Associates; WordStar, MicroPro International Corporation; Zork I, II, III, Infocom, Inc.

PHOTO ACKNOWLEDGMENTS

Figures 1.1, 1.2, 1.4, 1.6, 3.1, and 8.1 are courtesy of IBM corporation; figures 1.3, 10.1, and 10.2 are courtesy of WICO corporation; figure 10.5 is courtesy of Colby Computer; figures 1.8 and 10.4 are courtesy of Quadram corporation; figures 2.5, 2.6, 2.7, 2.12, 2.13, 2.14, and 2.15 are courtesy of Infocom, Inc.; figure 2.17 is courtesy of Executive Software Programming; figures 3.7, 3.8, and 8.9 are courtesy of Bausch & Lomb Houston Instruments Division; figure 3.10 is courtesy of Versa Computing, Inc.; figure 4.2 is courtesy of Proximity Devices Corporation; figure 3.8 is courtesy of Houston Instruments; figure 3.7 is courtesy of HIPLOT; figures 4.3, 4.4, 4.5, 4.6, 4.7, 4.8, 4.9, 4.10, and 4.11 are courtesy of Developmental Learning Materials; figures 4.12 and 4.13 are courtesy of Sunburst Communications, Inc.; figure 4.14 is courtesy of Lightning Software; figure 5.1 is courtesy of Continental Software; figure 6.1 is courtesy of Persoft, Inc.; figure 8.2 is courtesy of VisiCorp; figure 8.5 is courtesy of Lotus Development Corporation; figure 8.6 is courtesy of DesignWare, Inc.; figure 10.3 is courtesy of Logitech, Inc.

SIGNET, SIGNET CLASSIC, MENTOR, PLUME, MERIDIAN and NAL BOOKS are published by The New American Library, Inc.,
1633 Broadway, New York, New York 10019

First Printing, November, 1983

1 2 3 4 5 6 7 8 9

PRINTED IN THE UNITED STATES OF AMERICA

This book is the result of the creative efforts and research talent of the editorial staff at dilithium Press. The authors gratefully acknowledge the work of the staff and would like to publicly recognize each of the people who contributed to the creation of this book:

Nancy Morrice, *Senior Editor*

Deborrah Willis, *Editor*

Cleborne D. Maddux, *Technical Writer*

D. LaMont Johnson, *Technical Writer*

Jane Sterrett

Ann L. Hovland

Jo Anne Gilbert

Erin Lommen

Tamera Alen

Contents

CHAPTER ONE

Introducing the IBM Personal Computer

This book was written for people who own or are considering the purchase of an IBM PC or any of the computers that are compatible with the IBM PC. It shows you what can be done with a personal computer like the PC and gives detailed information on many of the programs that run on compatible computer systems.

The tremendous success of the IBM PC was not anticipated by many of the people in the personal computing field, including the authors of this book. Many people felt a company as large as IBM would have a hard time designing a good general-purpose computer thousands of people would buy. Others predicted the computer would be priced too high or that the computer would run only expensive IBM programs. Everyone was wrong. The IBM PC was an immediate hit, the computer works well, and there are thousands of programs for it.

IBM was the largest manufacturer of computers in the world even before it moved into the personal computer market. IBM's big multimillion dollar computers are known for their reliability, and the company has a reputation for supporting what it sells.

IBM didn't become an overnight success in the personal computer market because of a futuristic machine at the frontiers of technology, however. The machine is conservatively designed. Its success isn't due to a price so low smaller companies can't compete. Several computers run the same software as the IBM PC and cost hundreds of dollars less. The IBM PC is a hit because it is a solidly designed, reliable personal computer with lots of software available. It does everything well.

Figure 1.1　An IBM Personal Computer in the office

It plays excellent video games because it has color graphics and sound, it is a good word processing computer because it has an excellent keyboard and a high-capacity video display, and it is a good business computer because it is fast and has high-capacity (but optional) data storage systems. Of course, the millions IBM spent on advertising and the name IBM on the case didn't hurt sales either. Thousands of people have joined the *computer revolution* by placing an IBM PC on their desk at work or in the den at home.

This book tells you about many of the useful things a computer can do. It was written specifically for people who own or are considering the purchase of an IBM PC or an IBM PC compatible computer. The IBM PC is so popular many companies now manufacture computer systems that run the same programs as the IBM PC. Some use the same accessories and have exactly the same type of keyboard. The Columbia PC, Eagle PC, Toshiba PC, Sanyo 550, Corona PC, Osborne Executive (with optional equipment), Otrona, Seequa Chameleon, Sharp PC-5000, and many other models are, at least to some extent, compatible with the IBM PC. Thus if you own an IBM PC or any of the IBM compatible computers, this book provides information on many products you can use.

If you are not yet a computer owner, this book may also help you decide if you really want to buy one. This is one in a series on popular computer models. If you are shopping for a computer, you may want to read more than one book so you can compare the features and characteristics of several different models. This information will help you select the best computer for your needs.

WHAT'S IN THE REST OF THIS BOOK

Before a computer balances your checkbook or helps you beat back invading hordes of space no-good-niks, you will have to learn a bit about how it works and what it can do. In addition, you will quickly discover that there are many different ways of getting the computer to do a particular job. There are, for example, at least fifty good word processing programs for the IBM PC. There are hundreds of video games for it, some good, a few great ones, and many that can only be described as terrible. You won't want to buy everything that is available, but how do you decide? This book should help you make good decisions. It describes many of the programs you can get for the IBM PC. We assume that you aren't a computer expert but would like to know a lot more about how you can use an IBM PC in your office, home, or school. If you already own a PC, you may learn some new ways of using it while reading the chapters that follow this one. (We will use the letters PC to signify the IBM PC or a compatible computer.) Each chapter in *Things To Do with Your IBM Personal Computer* introduces you to one area of computer application. The chapters begin with some general background information. Then detailed information on programs or accessories for the PC is presented. This book won't make you a computer *expert*. Instead, it will help you become an informed consumer.

You can skip around in this book as much as you like. If

you are interested in video games, for example, you don't need to read the chapter on business applications. Here is a list of the chapters and a short description of their content:

Chapter One. *Introducing the IBM Personal Computer*. In this chapter you find out what a personal computer is and some ways you can use it. We also give you a brief guided tour of the IBM PC, and we introduce *software*.

Chapter Two. *Fun and Games*. This chapter describes the various recreational uses of the computer, with an emphasis on video games. It includes reviews of many of the most popular games.

Chapter Three. *Arts and Crafts*. You may not become a modern day Van Gogh or Bach, but there is more artistic potential in the computer than you might expect. It is more than a number cruncher! The IBM PC is an excellent arts and crafts computer. It has excellent color graphics and sound capabilities. There are some exciting music and visual arts programs.

Chapter Four. *The IBM PC as Teacher*. There are two aspects of educational computing: the use of the computer to teach other academic subjects and the computer as a topic of study itself. Several hundred programs for the PC teach everything from number recognition to chemistry. In addition, there are many books and programs that help you become *computer literate* on the PC.

Chapter Five. *Home Finance, Record Keeping, and Health Care*. Each year family finances become more complex and require more records. The time it takes to keep track of family finances can be cut drastically by computerizing some of these tasks. Several programs for the PC can help you with home finance and record keeping.

Chapter Six. *Tapping into the World: Telecommunications*. Did you know the PC sitting on your kitchen table can be used to communicate with computers all over the world? You can get all sorts of information, from Italian train schedules to reviews of the latest movies, when you use the PC as a telecommunications device.

Chapter Seven. *Word Processing*. It is possible to turn the

PC into a very sophisticated word processing system. The PC is an excellent computer for both home and professional or business word processing. With the right programs, a good printer, and some practice, your PC can rival word processing systems that cost four or five times the cost of this computer.

Chapter Eight. *Business and Professional Applications*. Regardless of your profession or the type of work you do, there is probably some aspect of it that could be improved or made more efficient by using a computer. This chapter is a brief overview of the ways a computer can be used on the job. It concludes with a description of some of the business software available.

Chapter Nine. *Programming*. Writing instructions that tell a computer what to do is called programming. Programming in the various languages available on the PC (for example, BASIC, PILOT, Logo) is described in this chapter.

Chapter Ten. *Peripherals*. The final chapter in the book deals with the accessories you can buy for the PC. Disk drives, printers, extra memory, video display circuits, and more are discussed in this chapter.

DO YOU HAVE TO LEARN TO PROGRAM YOUR COMPUTER?

You may have heard that you will have to learn to *program* the computer before it will do anything useful. While it's true your computer can't do anything without a program written in a computer language it understands, *you* don't have to write it.

Computer languages can take weeks or months to learn. Programs (software) that do complicated and useful things take time to write. Writing computer programs is an interesting hobby (or profession) thousands of people enjoy. You may decide you want to learn to write programs in a language like BASIC (Beginners All-purpose Symbolic Instruction Code). (We'll talk more about BASIC and other computer languages in Chapter 9.) Programming doesn't appeal to everyone who uses a computer, however. Fewer than ten percent of the people who own personal computers spend much of their time writing programs. The great majority of people do not write their own software. Instead, they buy software someone else has written. That's what we discuss in this book: readymade software for the PC. We'll tell you about software that lets the computer do hundreds of things, where to get the software, and the strengths and weaknesses we see in the software.

You can use your computer on many different levels. You may choose to regard your computer as you do any other appliance and simply use it as a labor-saving device. Or you may become fascinated with its internal workings and continue studying and learning about computers for the rest of your life.

This book is aimed primarily at those who want to use their computer as an appliance. If that is how you want to use yours, you won't have to learn too much computer jargon. The bad news is that you will have to learn a little jargon. You had to know a little jargon to learn to drive your car. Most of us learned the terms, concepts, and principles needed to drive a car as we were growing up. By the time we were teenagers, the automobile had become a necessity for most families. Common terms like ignition, premium gas, gas pedal, and brake were jargon when the automobile was first introduced. Today these terms are taken for granted. Jargon associated with the use of telephones has also become a part of our everyday language. The same thing will be true with computers. The next generation may well take for granted a computer on the dining table or in the recreation room. Kids will take terms like RAM and ROM in stride because they grew up with them and understand how to use computers. Unfortunately, we are part of a transitional generation. We didn't grow up with this inexpensive and useful technology. We are *automobile literate* and *telephone literate*, but we aren't *computer literate*. We'll try to help you solve this problem in three ways. First, as we introduce each computer term, we define it. Second, we have a little introduction to computer terms and concepts later on in this chapter. Third, there is a glossary in the back of the book.

HARDWARE AND SOFTWARE

Before we get into specifics, it is important that you understand two general computer terms. *Hardware* may conjure up visions of eggbeaters or pipe fittings, but it really refers to any piece of computer equipment. The computer itself is a piece of hardware, and so are other accessories like printers or disk drives (see Chapter Ten).

Software refers to the programs that make your computer do specific tasks. The mass media often make it seem very easy to make a computer do what you want it to. Television programs and movies often show people making a computer perform simply by talking to it. As you may have already discovered, your computer isn't that friendly yet. (Actually, we talk to our computers all the time, usually when they don't do what we want, and what we say is often x-rated!). Communicating with a computer today usually involves typing instructions on its keyboard or transferring information stored electronically on a *cassette* or *disk* into the electronic memory of the computer. The instructions a computer follows when it performs a particular task are called *software*. It takes software to make hardware useful.

OH, NO! JARGON!

It's not as bad as all that. We're just going to give you a little guided tour of jargon, as well as an introduction to the IBM PC. Figure 1.1 is a block diagram of the IBM PC's hardware. The least expensive model of the PC includes the power supply, keyboard, cassette I/O, and the main CPU circuit board (called the system board). You need several more items just to get the computer to work (for instance, a video display), and many people end up spending two to five times as much on options as they do on the basic IBM PC. That is because the computer is an *unbundled* system. Many items, such as printer interfaces and the video display, are extra-cost options on the IBM PC. Instead of buying a system with everything you need to start computing, IBM sells a bare bones system and lets you select the options you want. For example, both a black and white and a color display system are available. You buy the one you want.

The Power Supply

The basic system includes the main system unit, which houses a CPU circuit board, memory, expansion slots where

**Figure 1.2   The IBM Personal Computer with
single disk drive and video monitor**

**Figure 1.3   This IBM interface card from WICO
allows you to add a joystick or trackball.**

accessories can be plugged in, and the power supply. The first two disk drives are also installed in the system unit. IBM's attention to detail shows in its well-designed power supply. It is behind the disk drives and is completely enclosed in a metal case to reduce interference with television reception and to provide an extra margin of safety.

Figure 1.4   IBM's Personal Computer expansion unit lets you add more cards.

I/O Ports

I/O is an abbreviation for input/output. If a computer is to be of any use, it must be able to communicate with you. This basic function is called input/output. The places on the computer circuit board where I/O occurs are often called *ports*. The IBM PC has several standard ports that allow you to communicate with it. The keyboard at the back of the computer is the primary means of entering data and instructions to the computer.

Most computers also have standard ports for connecting a cassette recorder or disk drive, as well as ports for a printer and a video display. The IBM PC has only a cassette recorder port and a keyboard port. All other ports are extra-cost options.

There are also five expansion slots on the main circuit board of the standard IBM PC. (There are eight in the IBM PC-XT.) If you want to connect a printer to your computer you must buy a plug-in card (called an expansion or interface card) that has either serial or a parallel I/O port on it. Many types of cards from IBM and from at least a hundred other companies can be plugged into the expansion slots. Virtually anything made to attach to a computer can be connected to an IBM PC with one of these interface cards. Joysticks and game paddles, for example, can be added to the PC, if you have an optional interface card.

If you end up with more than five accessory cards, an expansion chassis is available that connects to the main system unit and lets you add more cards. IBM and several other companies, such as Techmar, make expansion chassis for the PC.

Keyboard

The PC's keyboard is a very controversial unit. It is a well engineered, detachable unit with eighty-three keys. There is a set of ten programmable function keys on the left side of the unit. A function key sends the computer an instruction to do something, backspace and tab, for example. Programmable function keys can serve different functions in different programs. One of the PC's programmable function keys might cause the computer to delete a word or sentence when you are using a word processing program. The same key might tell the computer to perform a particular calculation in an accounting program. The ten programmable function keys on the PC make it much easier to learn complex programs. All ten are located on the left side of the keyboard. That's great for left handed people, but right handers may find the location less than desirable. Cursor control keys let you move the cursor, a rectangle of light that tells you where you are on the screen. The PC's cursor control keys are actually part of the numeric keypad. Some keys serve a dual purpose as number keys and cursor control keys.

The keyboard makes a rather loud click when a key is

pressed. Some people find that annoying. Many more complain about the placement of some of the keys. The left shift key, for example, is one key position further out than it is on a regular typewriter keyboard. There is a \ key where you expect to find the shift key. The RETURN key is also one key further out than it is on most keyboards. In its place is a tilde (-) key. The RETURN key has a regular size top. On most keyboards that key, one of the most frequently used, is oversized.

Keys that change the operation of the keyboard (for example, shift lock keys) do not lock down when pressed and do not have indicator lights to tell you when they are on.

IBM maintains they have an excellent keyboard that was developed after considerable research. We dislike the keyboard, and so do many other IBM PC owners. Fortunately,

Figure 1.5   A replacement keyboard for the IBM PC

there are some solutions to the design flaws in the IBM PC keyboard. Some are inexpensive overlays that do things like change the size of the RETURN key. Vertex Systems has one called the Keyfixer ($20) that enlarges the RETURN key, the TAB, and two shift keys.

Several companies solve the keyboard problem with a complete replacement keyboard. Keytronic, a respected manufacturer of quality keyboards, sells a keyboard that replaces the one on the PC for around $235. It has lights on the shift lock keys, a properly located left shift key, and TAB and RETURN keys with those names on them instead of little arrows. Colby Computer also has a replacement keyboard for $260. The Colby unit puts the left shift key in the right place, adds four cursor control keys on the top left of the keyboard, uses red lights to indicate when a shift key is locked down, and arranges the programmable function keys across the top.

Another interesting keyboard accessory is the PC-Documate keyboard templates from SMA. The PC's programmable function keys are simply labelled F1 through F10. These templates fit around the keyboard and provide labels that tell you what the various keys do when you run popular programs. The templates are $15 each and are available for programs like *WordStar*, *VisiCalc*, *Multiplan*, *SuperCalc*, *EasyWriter II*, *dBase II*, and BASIC. There is even a custom template you can label yourself. This is a handy accessory that makes learning some of the more complicated programs much easier.

Video Display

If you buy the basic stripped-down IBM PC, you don't get any of the video circuits. IBM has two different display cards that plug into the expansion slots. One is a monochrome display card. The video display generated by this circuit has no color and limited graphics. The other option, the Color/Graphics Monitor Adapter, lets you create outstanding color graphics. If you add an optional RF modulator to the system, you can use an ordinary color television as a video display. However, few people do that, because the computer is capable of generating much better video output than an ordinary television can display. Most people elect to use an ordinary color video monitor or a special RGB color monitor. RGB stands for Red, Green, Blue. RBG monitors can produce brilliant, detailed color graphics when connected to the IBM PC, but they cost between $500 and $1000. Ordinary color monitors do a nice job and cost between $250 and $700.

Both the monochrome and the color cards can display text. The format used is 25 lines of 80 characters, a very desirable format for business and professional applications. By offering two types of display cards, IBM has created an unfortunate dilemma for many buyers. If you want high quality color graphics, a strong point of this computer, you must get the color card. Many people feel the text displayed by this card is hard to read, however, while the text display of the monochrome card is clean and crisp. Instead of buying a video display card from IBM, you may want to get one from another source. Several companies sell display cards for the PC that let you use monochrome and color display formats interchangeably without buying two different cards.

IBM also sells a monochrome video monitor and a color monitor for the PC. However, these are standard products, and monitors from at least fifty other suppliers will also work well with the PC.

The display of ordinary text is sometimes called *alphanumeric display* because it is made up of letters and numbers.

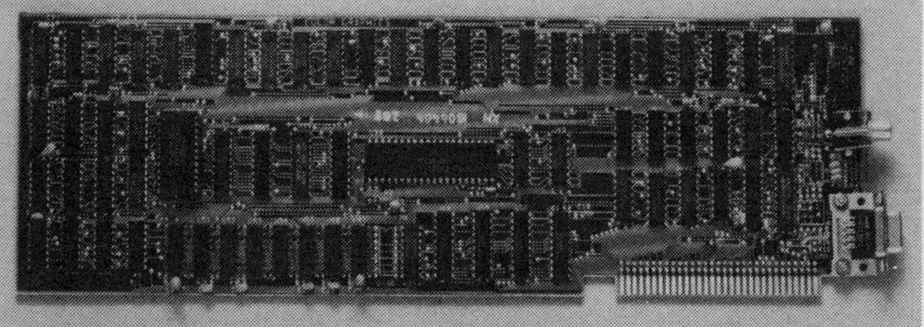

**Figure 1.6   To display high-quality color graphics,
a color card is needed.**

The IBM PC is also capable of displaying graphs, figures, and illustrations. If the video monitor has a picture of an ocean with a ship riding at anchor on a blue sky summer day, you have a *graphics display*. What you see on the screen is composed of special graphics characters. High-quality graphics displays that show fine detail are made up of tiny dots of color called *picture elements* or *pixels*. The IBM PC can create high-quality pictures and figures made up of thousands of tiny colored pixels. Graphics of this type are called *high-resolution* or *HI-RES* graphics.

Sound

The PC has a built-in speaker and can generate simple musical sounds as well as sound effects. You can even create your own sound effects by writing a program in BASIC that tells the computer what sounds to generate through the speaker.

Memory

When you press a key on the keyboard or load a program into the computer from a cassette or disk, there must be somewhere to put that information. Each letter you type in is converted to a code and stored in the memory of the computer. All computers convert characters into ones and zeros (on and off electrical signals). The letter A, for example, has the code 01000001. Such a set of eight digits is called a *byte*, and each of the ones and zeros is called a *bit*. Seven of those bits are used to define the code for each character the PC understands. The eighth is usually added to the character code so the computer can check for errors. This process, called *parity checking*, will not be discussed here. Bytes, the eight-bit patterns, are the fundamental code units for the PC and for most small computers.

Every letter, digit, graphic symbol, and punctuation mark the PC understands has a unique code that is one byte. There is not a place in the computer where an A or B or 7 or + is stored. Instead, each of those symbols has its own one-byte code. This code is what is stored in the memory of the computer.

The PC comes with at least 104,000 bytes of memory, but not all of it is available for general use. There are actually two different types of memory in the IBM PC: RAM and ROM. ROM stands for *Read Only Memory*. This type of memory is generally programmed at the factory, and its contents cannot be changed by the user. A little over 40,000 bytes of ROM are in the IBM PC. The instructions that allow the computer to understand a version of BASIC, a popular computer language, are in ROM. When the cassette-only version of the IBM PC is turned on, it automatically goes to the section of ROM where the instructions for BASIC are stored and prepares itself to work with commands given it in BASIC. If you have a PC with disk drives, the computer follows instructions in its ROM that let it load in programs stored on disks.

Not all computer memory can be ROM, however. Much of the memory in the IBM PC is RAM, or *Random Access Memory*. RAM is general-purpose memory available for use by the computer operator. Early versions of the PC came with just over 16,000 bytes of RAM, but current models have a minimum of 65,536 bytes. There are sockets on the main circuit board that let you plug in enough memory chips to provide 262,144 bytes of RAM. If you need more RAM, plug-in RAM cards will expand RAM to over 600,000 bytes. That is quite a bit of RAM. Few applications need more than 128,000 bytes of RAM.

Computer buffs generally do not talk about memory in terms of bytes. Memory is usually described in K. Each K of memory is 1024 bytes. Thus 16K would be 1024 times 16 or 16,384 bytes. Just multiply the number of K by 1024 to determine the number of bytes of memory.

The CPU

The CPU, or *Central Processing Unit*, is the heart of a computer system. The CPU is the chip that actually processes data; most of the other components in the computer support or assist the CPU as it does its work.

Although most CPUs are smaller than a half dollar, the electronic components they contain would have filled a room a few decades ago. Large scale integration technology permits manufacturers to cram thousands of circuits into tiny silicon chips that work dependably and use less power than an electric razor.

The IBM PC uses an 8088 microprocessor chip. This chip is a hybrid type that processes data sixteen bits at a time. The 8088 stores data in memory in bytes (eight bits), but it processes data in sixteen-bit groups. That makes it much faster than microprocessor chips like the Z80 that process data in eight-bit units.

Faster operation is one of the advantages of the 8088, but it is probably not the most important advantage. Microprocessor chips must be designed to use a certain maximum amount of memory. The Z80, for example, is normally capable of using no more than 64K of memory (both RAM and ROM). When the Z80 was designed, memory was expensive. Today memory is cheap and many applications, such as color graphics, word processing and electronic spreadsheets, need lots of memory. The 8088 can *address* or use over a million characters of memory. The ability to use large amounts of memory is a very desirable feature.

A chip named the 8086 is compatible with the 8088, but uses sixteen bits throughout. It is even faster than the 8088, but computers that use it are more expensive to design and build. IBM thus elected to use a very good CPU, the 8088, but not the most expensive chip of its type.

Mass Storage

Random access memory serves as temporary storage for data or program information while a program is running. Programs and data in RAM are lost when the computer is switched off, however. A functional computer system must, therefore, have some way to store programs and data permanently for later use. The IBM PC comes with the circuits needed to use an ordinary cassette recorder to store programs and data. However, cassette storage is slow and not very reliable, and very few IBM owners use it. Over ninety-nine percent of the software for the PC assumes you have at least one floppy disk drive. A disk system provides you with reliable, high-speed storage. Several versions of the 5¼-inch disk drives are available for the PC. All use floppy disks—round, flexible plastic platters enclosed in a protective case—to store information. You insert one of the floppy disks in a disk drive, and the computer can magnetically store data on the disk or read data previously stored on the disk. When you buy a program on a floppy disk, the instructions the computer needs to run that program are stored as magnetic codes on the disk. To run the program, you tell the computer to load those instructions into RAM.

Figure 1.7   Floppy disk

Floppy disk drives come in several different flavors. Some store data on only one side of the disk, some store it on both. The least expensive disk drives for the IBM PC store data on one side. These can put up to 160K of data on each disk. Higher-priced drives use both sides of a disk and store 320K of data. We strongly suggest you buy the 320K versions if you plan to use the computer for professional or business uses.

Two disk drives can be installed in the main system unit. Two more can be added outside the computer. They connect to the system unit through a cable. The basic PC does not have the ability to use disk drives, however. You must buy a disk drive interface card that plugs into one of the expansion slots in the system unit. The disk drives then plug into it. Several companies sell disk drive interface cards and disk drives that will work on the IBM PC.

The IBM PC-XT comes with one floppy disk and one *hard disk* built into the case. Hard disk drives are very fast, high-capacity systems that store data on a spinning metal platter. The hard disk on the XT stores ten *megabytes* of data. A megabyte is 1000 times 1024 or 1,024,000 bytes. Several companies other than IBM make hard disk systems for the IBM PC. Corona and Corvus are only two of at least twenty manufacturers of PC-compatible hard disk drives.

Software

The IBM PC speaks BASIC because a version of BASIC is in ROM. Another version of BASIC comes with the disk drive system. Called BASICA, this is the version of BASIC that is normally considered IBM BASIC. If you buy a program that requires BASIC, that usually refers to BASICA and not the cassette-only BASIC in ROM.

Computers are made up of many components such as memory, keyboard, display, and disk drives. A special type of software called an *operating system* is required to make all these components work together. In a computer that has disk drives, this software is called a *Disk Operating System* or *DOS*. The system IBM selected for their computer was developed by Microsoft and is called MSDOS (MicroSoft Disk Operating System) when used on other computers. IBM calls it PCDOS. Perhaps because IBM selected MSDOS, it is now the most popular disk operating system for computers that use the 8088 CPU. Another disk operating system, CP/M86, also works with the PC. It was developed by Digital Research, another well-known software company. Digital Research created CP/M80, by far the most popular operating system on business computers that use the Z80 CPU. CP/M86 is a version of CP/M for 16-bit computers such as the 8088. A few programs for the IBM PC will run only if you have CP/M86. However, most can be purchased in a version that will run under the control of MSDOS.

Although disk operating systems are necessary, they are not interesting in themselves. The interesting aspect of IBM PC software is the *applications* software: programs that let you do something useful, such as keeping track of inventory, balancing your books, or playing a fast-paced video game.

Put simply, the software base of the IBM PC is second to none. More good software for more types of applications has been written for the IBM PC than for any other computer in the world, with the possible exception of the Apple II. Since Quadram Corporation sells an interface card that lets you run

Figure 1.8   The QUADLINK: an interface card that allows Apple II software to run on the IBM PC.

Apple II software on the IBM PC, we can confidently say that more software will run on the IBM PC than any other computer, bar none. There is even an expansion card called Baby Blue that lets you run programs designed for computers that use CP/M80.

If you are new to computing, you may not realize how important lots of software is to a computer owner. Hardware is useless without software. Some computers have fewer than 50 programs that will run on them. Others have lots of software, but it is concentrated in one area, like video games or sophisticated business software. The IBM PC has it all, from video games with beautiful, animated color graphics to outstanding business software. If the computer has an area where software is thin, it is in the educational area. The Apple II clearly has more programs in that area, but each week brings announcements of more educational programs for the IBM PC. You are fortunate to have a computer with so much software.

OWNER RESOURCES

There are many resources for anyone who buys an IBM PC computer. Literally hundreds of good books have been written on the IBM PC. You can get many introductory books, books like this one that review software, books on programming in BASIC, books on CP/M86 and PCDOS, and much more.

Several magazines focus exclusively on the IBM PC and compatible computers. At least five are currently available, and most of the general interest personal computer magazines, like *Personal Computing* and *Creative Computing*, also publish some articles on the PC. We will describe three outstanding magazines for PC owners below:

PC ($20 for 12 issues) was one of the first magazines for PC owners. It is a fat monthly publication filled with ads and articles about the PC. The magazine publishes tutorial articles on many aspects of PC usage, as well as reviews of accessories, peripherals, and software. This is one of the better publications. *PC*'s original editor was David Bunnell. Bunnell and a group of energetic editors began *PC* with financial backing from a New York software distributor. Bunnell understood that he and some of his senior editors would get a share of ownership in the magazine when it was established. They worked long hours at relatively low pay to get the magazine on its feet. Their efforts produced an outstanding magazine, perhaps the best of its type.

The person who put up the money for this magazine decided to sell it in 1982 and began negotiations with several potential buyers. Eventually it was sold to Ziff-Davis, a company with a large stable of computer magazines, and Bunnell arrived at work one morning to find his offices locked. Ziff-Davis and the person who sold the magazine took the position that Bunnell did not have rights to any percentage of ownership. Ziff-Davis therefore considered itself to own 100 percent of the magazine. Bunnell was told he could continue working for *PC* but under a new contract developed by Ziff-Davis.

Bunnell talked to Pat McGovern, owner of another publishing company. McGovern's company owns *InfoWorld*, an outstanding weekly publication on the personal computing field. The upshot of Bunnell's conversations with McGovern was a wholesale resignation at *PC*. Bunnell and over twenty of his staff left the magazine and started a new magazine called *PC World*.

PC World (15 issues for $24) is another fat, informative magazine for IBM PC owners. It uses a format similar to *PC* and publishes the same mix of articles: tutorials, reviews of hardware and software, and discussions of general concepts or issues. Some people consider *PC World* to be the continuation of the original *PC*. In any case, these are two outstanding magazines filled with information of interest to PC owners. We recommend both.

PC Tech Journal (6 issues for $20) is the newest of the three magazines. Like *PC*, it is a Ziff-Davis publication. *PC Tech Journal* is a more specialized publication written primarily for experienced computer users, particularly those who are interested in writing programs for the IBM PC. With titles like *How to Choose a C Compiler*, *Computer Generated Stereo-*

scopic Images, and *The Anatomy and Construction of XB*, you can see that the magazine is somewhat specialized. It is an excellent resource for people who want the type of information it publishes, however.

CHAPTER TWO

Games and Entertainment

OK, so you finally made the big decision. You signed your life away to the finance company and brought home your IBM computer with all the accessories. You've astounded your friends (and appeased your spouse, or tried to) by demonstrating how it analyzes real estate investments, improves your child's spelling, and stores your favorite recipe for chocolate-covered cabbage. That's great. Now that the friends have gone home and everyone is in bed, it's time to get down to business. Time to put your computer through its paces. Time for what you *really* bought your IBM for: playing computer games!

A Word of Caution

We have not attempted to review every, or even most, of the games available today for the IBM PC. First, there are too many of them, and quite a few are so poor they do not deserve mention. It would take an entire book to review all the bad software for the PC, and for that reason we decided to use this space to describe software we found at least acceptable, if not excellent. Even with this limitation, we were not able to describe all the good software. We hope this chapter will at least give you an idea of the type of recreational software you can find for the PC.

THE IBM IS A GOOD GAME COMPUTER

If you have ever played an arcade game, you know that much of their appeal lies in colorful, imaginative graphics and sound. Graphics and sound features are strong points on the PC, and many programmers have taken advantage of those features to design excellent recreational programs.

Currently there are several hundred video games that run on the IBM PC. The PC still has fewer than there are for the ATARI, Commodore 64, or Apple II computers. There are a couple of reasons for this. First, the IBM PC has been marketed primarily as a business machine. Then, too, although the PC has the potential for outstanding color graphics, many PCs have none. IBM lets buyers select between a monochrome and a color display card. Many people select the monochrome card so they can use inexpensive video monitors. However, PCs with the monochrome card can't run many of the programs described in this chapter, because they need the graphics/color adaptor card and a high-resolution color monitor. Color graphics aren't needed to play every kind of computer game, but color makes a game more appealing.

Software companies and independent game programmers are quick to realize that people who buy the IBM PC play as well as work. In 1983, over 200 games for the PC were announced. By the time you read this there may be over a thousand games for the PC.

TYPES OF GAMES FOR THE IBM

We will discuss computer games on the IBM computer in the following categories: action games; fantasy games; simulation games; card games, Las Vegas-style games, and board games; and sports games.

Action Video Games

Action video games, or arcade-type games, emphasize sophisticated animated graphics and sound effects. Many of the video games for the PC are adaptations of arcade games that have earned millions of dollars, a quarter at a time, for their developers.

Almost all the popular video games are *real time* games. That is, things are happening on the screen whether you do anything or not. Doing nothing is generally disastrous and quick response times are highly rewarded. Whereas adventure games call for careful thought and analysis, arcade style games are mostly action. You can quickly learn the rules of these games, but you earn high points if you can respond quickly and accurately to changing events on the video screen. Manual dexterity, fine motor skills, and the ability to coordinate visual information with fine motor responses (for example, to aim and fire the photon torpedoes at rapidly approaching Klingons) are all essential ingredients of high calibre video game play.

Some countries have outlawed video games on the grounds that they lead children into all sorts of bad habits. That seems a bit silly to us. Like almost anything else, video game playing probably could crowd out other healthy experiences children need to develop properly. That seems unlikely in most cases. In addition, the skills developed playing video games and adventure simulations may be useful in other areas. Some therapists who work with dyslexic and learning disabled children, for example, use standard or specially designed video games to help children develop better visual-motor coordination. The problem-solving practice provided by adventure simulations is much like that in many programs designed to stimulate creativity and improve children's cognitive abilities. However, it would be difficult, to convince the IRS that the $300 you spent on video games last year was a medical expense. Enjoyment is the primary reason for playing video games.

Spyder

Spyder is a one-player action game available on disk for $39.95 from Mirror Images Software, Inc. To play this game, you'll need at least 64K of RAM and the color/graphics adapter. This is a typical action game with a little bit of a new twist. As a bevy of creepy spiders (spelled *Spyders*, for some reason) descend on webs from the top of the screen, your job is to blast them from below. You're equipped with a laser gun (spelled *lazer*, undoubtedly for the same reason that *spider* is spelled *Spyder*). You can blow them away with your gun, but it won't fire in any direction except up. An added problem is that your laser/lazer has a limited charge. When it runs low, a warning tone sounds, and you have to move over to an energy pack to recharge.

So if the spiders reach the ground before you get them, what's your only alternative? Tromping on them, of course. If you don't, it's curtains. You can move your cartoon-figure man to the right or left to squash the little buggers.

Not for the squeamish, right? It gets even messier in the more difficult levels of the game. A little pair of scissors sometimes shoots across the top of the display, cutting the webs and causing the spiders to fall to the ground. They head right for you, of course, so you'll be busy squashing them with your clod-hoppers. If you don't do your tarantella efficiently enough, the dastardly little devils get you. First they dance a fiendish jig, and then they spin you up in a red web. The flesh-crawling finish comes when the screen fills up entirely with spiders. What a way to go!

This is an excellent action game with a couple of nice touches. The program keeps score for you. You win points when you blast or stomp a spider, lose them if you fire and miss. The game keeps a record of high scores. If you have terminal hand-cramp or some other emergency, you can stop the game temporarily, then resume where you left off.

Flipperball

Flipperball is an excellent pinball simulation available for $29.95 from Distributed Software Systems. You will need 64K of memory and the color/graphics adapter.

The graphics and sound effects are excellent in this popular game. The left side of the screen pictures the playing board of a traditional-looking pinball machine. The right side shows the score, the player, and the balls remaining.

The game incorporates all the standard pinball equipment. There are eight lanes at the top of the screen that any ball can roll through. There are three very sensitive bumpers in the center of play. When the ball hits them, it rebounds with realistic pinball sound effects. If you tire of the sound effects, you can have silent play by pressing the F1 key.

Flipperball includes bumpers, flippers, and magnetic roll-overs. You can even vary the force of the plunger that sends each ball out onto the playing surface.

The outstanding part of this game is the realistic ball movement. It's easy to forget that it's all electronic and that gravity really has nothing to do with the action. Our only objection is that the ball looks almost square instead of round. This is a minor problem, however.

If you're a pinball wizard (or want to be), you'll like this game.

The Chrome Ranger

The Chrome Ranger is a very good maze game in the *PAC-MAN* look-a-like category. You will need 64K and the color/graphics adapter. Game adapter and joysticks can be used but are not required, and the game is available from Omniware for $29.95.

This game uses the standard *PAC-MAN* action. You direct the Chrome Ranger, complete with munching sound effects, around a maze. You eat up various little dots and attempt to avoid the nasties on your trail. If you can eat up one of the

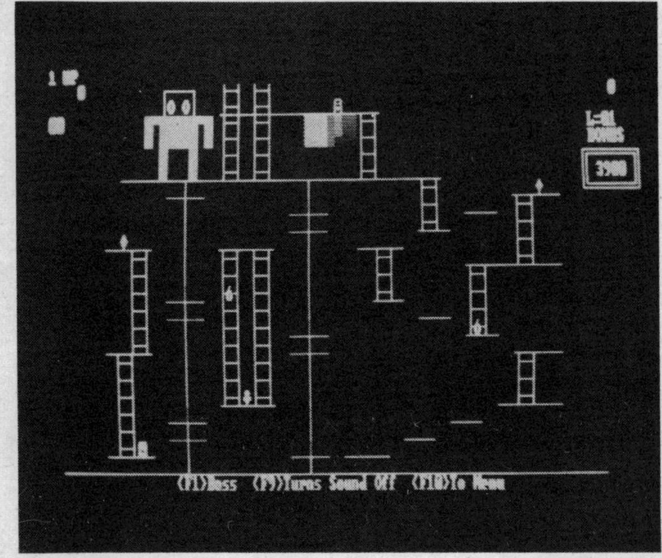

Figure 2.1   Gorilla

magic little thing-a-ma-jigs scattered about the maze, you can briefly turn the tables on the nasties and eat them.

You can turn the sound off if you choose, and there are three levels of difficulty. If you are addicted to *PAC-MAN*, the *Chrome Ranger* will give a quick fix.

PC Arcade

At $49.95, *PC Arcade* is a bargain; it has ten different game programs. This package published by FriendlySoft will probably be a hit, since it has so many programs and will run on the standard IBM PC, with or without color.

Then, too, most of the programs are passing-fair imitations of popular arcade-style action games. Programs include *Gorilla, ASCII Man, Starfighter, Frogger, Robot War, Shooter, Bug Blaster, Brick Breaker*, and *Eagle Lander*. These games resemble such favorites as *Donkey Kong, PAC-MAN, Defender, Frogger, Berserk, Attack, Centipede, Breakout*, and

Lunar Lander. In addition, you get an enjoyable horse racing game called *PC Derby*.

An interesting touch of this package is called *the-boss-is-coming* feature. If you suddenly press F1, the game disappears and a very business-like, but nondescript bar graph appears. When you press F1 again, the game comes back. Efficiency experts beware, here comes *PC Arcade*!

Snake

Snake is a type-it-yourself free game by Peter Quinn. It's listed in the March 1983 issue of *PC World* magazine. *Snake* doesn't include sophisticated graphics and high-resolution color, but the price is right. You buy the magazine and type the program in.

When the game begins, two snakes appear on the screen. The snakes are really just lines on your display. One of these lines is solid. You're the solid line. The other is a dotted line,

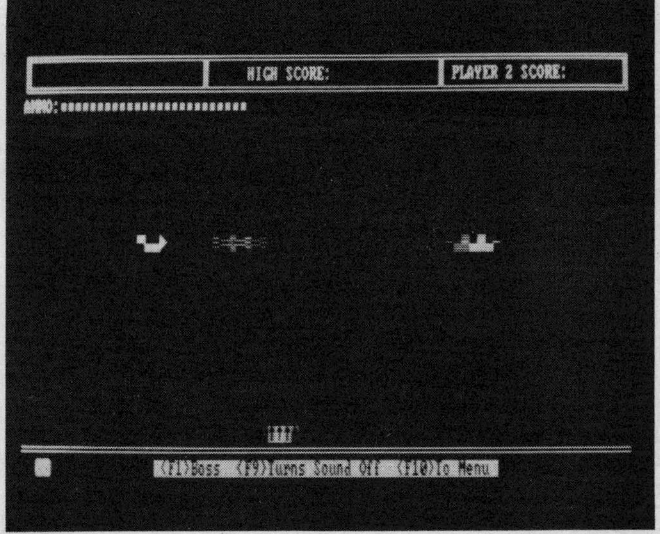

Figure 2.2   Starfighter

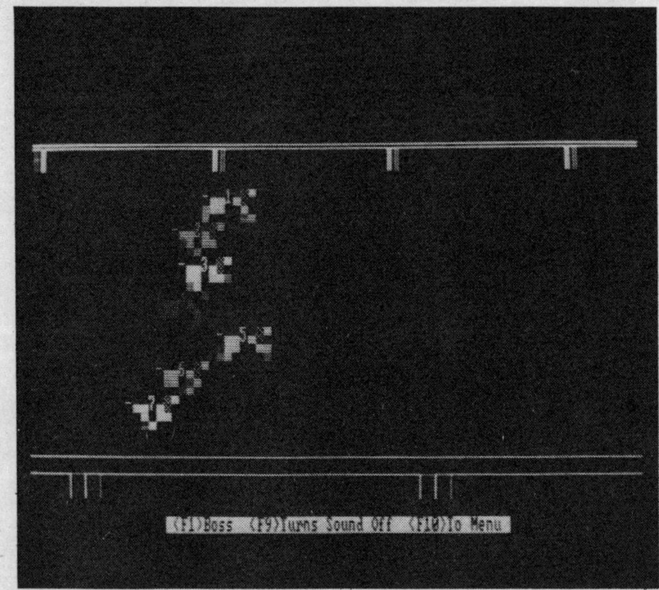

Figure 2.3 PC Derby

and that snake is the computer snake. Both snakes begin to grow at a steady rate. You can control the direction your snake grows, but you have no control over the computer snake. The loser of the game is the first snake to run into anything at all: screen boundaries, its own body, or the other snake. What you must do is maneuver your snake into a position that causes the computer snake to run into something. If you do that, you win. The computer works against you, of course, trying to impose the same fate on your snake.

This game is typical of the free games printed in computer magazines. There's a catch, of course—to get this game free, you'll have to type in the entire program (approximately seventy-five lines). This is time-consuming, and if you make errors, the game will not perform properly. Nevertheless, there is satisfaction in getting an enjoyable game for nothing, even if it takes some effort.

Adventure Games

The development of adventure games on the computer is credited to Will Crowther and Don Woods who, in the seventies, created a game called *Adventure* which ran on the DEC PDP-11 computer at Stanford University in California. Adventure games are strategy-oriented. You must think your way through rather that act your way through. Excellent eye/hand coordination, fast reflexes, and good peripheral vision are all essential ingredients for success on most of the arcade video games that use joysticks or game paddles. But you don't need these attributes for most adventure games. Many of the adventure games don't have graphics displays but rely primarily on text displayed on the screen. A game is likely to begin with a paragraph that sets the scene for the game: *You are standing on the edge of a forest. There is a narrow winding road that*

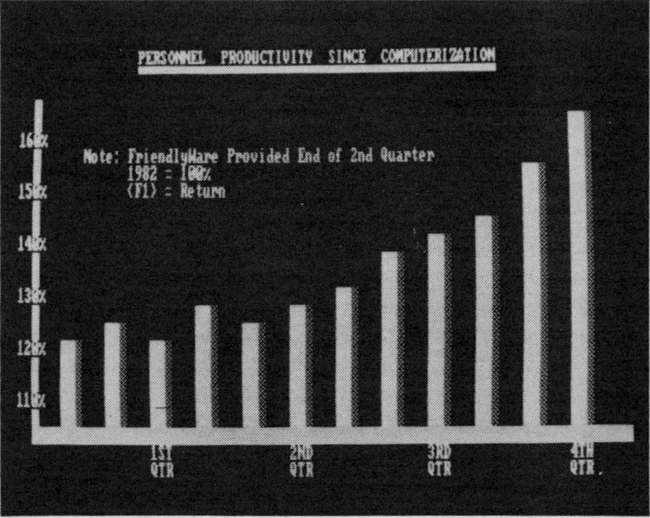

Figure 2.4   The bar graph that appears if "the boss is coming"

leads out of the forest and winds through the hills to a large stone house, shrouded in fog, which stands on the edge of a cliff.

All adventure games put you in an environment (forest, cave with many chambers, castle with many rooms, maze), give you a task to perform (stay alive, get out, find the treasure, rescue the prisoners), and put all sorts of dangers in your way (monsters, cliffs, sorcerers, enemy soldiers, bombs). Two final ingredients of an adventure are incomplete information and ways of getting that information. That means you must begin the adventure without all the information you need to deal with the situation. However, the game gives you ways to learn more about the game's environment and about how to deal successfully with the adventure. In most adventures you move about through a series of rooms. The term room really refers to different segments of the game, such as rooms, cities, chambers in a cave, and so on.

Adventure games let you move about the rooms by giving the computer instructions (for instance, GO AHEAD, TURN LEFT, CLIMB STAIRS, DIG OUT). Depending on the adventure, it may understand only a few instructions or several hundred. Some games even let you create your own characters and move them about independently. You can endow the characters with different powers and send them against foes they are likely to overcome (for instance, a sorcerer against a wicked magician, and a powerful Samson type against a giant). However, things do not always work out as you hope, and it is not unusual to lose some of your characters.

Playing adventure games is not something everyone enjoys. Some games take several hours, even days, to learn, and playing a complete game through to its conclusion is likely to take at least ten hours, if not longer. Because they take quite a bit of time, some of the hundreds of adventure games available today have provisions for saving your position in the game. You can play for several hours today, save the game at that point, and resume play later at the point where you stopped. If you like strategy, enjoy solving intricate puzzles, and have time to devote to the task, playing adventure games can be a pleasant addiction. Here is how the beginning of a typical adventure game set in a magic castle might go:

You are in the chapel of the castle with a closed coffin nearby. The computer asks, *What shall I do now*? You have several one and two-word commands you can give the computer. If you type E and press the RETURN key, the computer takes this as an instruction to go east. The computer responds with *O.K.*. Here is how the adventure might proceed. The instructions you give are in lowercase, while the computer's response is in uppercase.

O.K.
1 (the instruction for LOOK)
I'M IN A TUNNEL. BLOODY KNIFE. MASSIVE STONE DOOR WITH A SAPPHIRE SET INTO IT.
WEST (this means you can only proceed west from this point)
I SEE NOTHING VERY SPECIAL.
WHAT SHALL I DO NOW?

w

O.K.
WHAT SHALL I DO NOW?

1

I'M IN A CHAPEL. CLOSED COFFIN.
NORTH, SOUTH, EAST, WEST (you can proceed in these directions from this point)

get coffin

BEYOND MY POWER TO DO THAT
WHAT SHALL I DO NOW?

open coffin

O.K.

enter coffin

THERE'S NO ROOM IN THERE FOR ME!

examine coffin

A SIGN HERE SAYS: COUNT CRISTO'S BEEN CURSED! THERE'S ONE WAY FOR HIM TO FLEE! FIND IT, AND HE'LL GO FREE. THERE'S A MAN HERE WEARING A SAPPHIRE RING.

north

O.K.

WINDOW JUST SLAMMED SHUT

This is how an adventure might begin. There are many instructions most adventure programs understand, such as climb, drop, enter, examine, leave, light, look, move, pull, push, read, take, get, wear. If you find something you think will be useful later, you could tell the computer to get that object (for example, GET SWORD). Later you can type I and get an inventory of everything you are carrying. Most adventures have several dangerous sections. If you pick up the wrong things, they can kill you, and if you enter the wrong area, you can be trapped there forever. Both hostile and helpful beings are usually scattered about, and you can get powerful magic to help you overcome obstacles.

The instructions that come with most adventures recommend strongly that you make a map of your travels through the rooms. Unless you have an excellent memory, it is almost impossible to master this adventure without a map, because there are so many rooms to explore and so many dead ends or dangers to avoid.

Most of the early fantasy or adventure games (and many current programs) were *text-only* games that used no graphics. The player actually read the entire game, selecting certain options as the game went on. Typical of this type of game is *Adventure* from Microsoft.

Adventure

Adventure is a version of a popular early adventure game called *Colossal Cave*. This is the only game that IBM sells, and it goes for $30. There are no graphics or sound effects, but if you like adventure games, you are sure to enjoy this one.

The object of the game is to enter Colossal Cave and carry off the fifteen treasures hidden there. There are puzzles to be solved and all the other standard adventure game scenarios.

If you get trapped in a room and seem to have no way out, the program gives you a hint. You must pay by giving up points. You acquire points by successfully exploring rooms and by gathering treasure. You may save a game after you have begun and resume it later where you left off. Both children and adults will enjoy this historic piece of game software.

Zork I, II, and III

The *Zork* adventure games from Infocom have enjoyed fantastic popularity. These wonderful adventure games are available for most small computers and sell for $39.95 each. Their claim to fame is the large vocabulary and complicated syntax the program understands. You aren't limited to the two-word commands of most traditional adventure games. The *Zork* trilogy understands complex, lengthy sentences. The plot resembles most adventure games, with trolls, magical items, and treasures galore. But this series of games is a real pleasure to talk to. The programs seem almost human!

If you have problems solving the puzzles presented in the *Zork* games, you may be interested in purchasing *Invisiclues*. This is a clever book of clues written in invisible ink. The clues become visible when rubbed with a special pen supplied with the package.

In *Zork I* you seek the Twenty Treasures of Zork and attempt to escape with your life. In *Zork II*, the Wizard of Frobozz takes you deeper into the underground kingdom where you

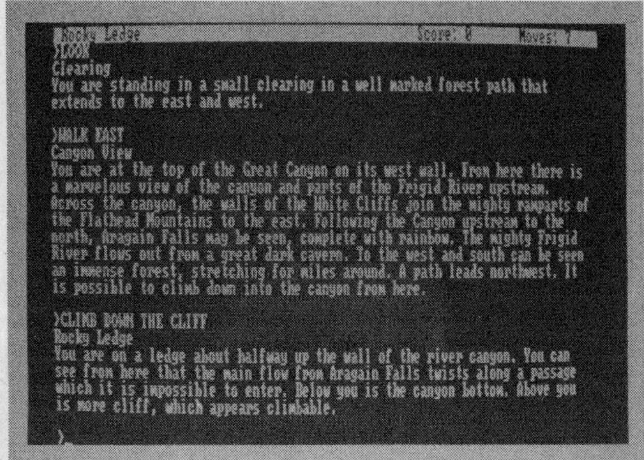

Figure 2.5   Zork I

meet the Wizard himself. You may not survive the meeting! In *Zork III*, you will meet the Dungeon Master, the most dangerous opponent of all.

The *Zork* games are classics, and should not be missed by anyone who likes fantasy-adventure games. These are the top of the line in text-only games.

Temple of Apshai

Temple of Apshai is a popular adventure game that may represent the wave of the future in fantasy-adventure games. The game has some of your characteristics of classic action games and some of the characteristics of more typical fantasy games. *Temple of Apshai* sells for $39.95 (Automated Simulations).

Like many adventure games, you begin by equipping your character with weapons and provisions. Unlike the early adventure games, you eventually see your character depicted on the screen in animated graphics. In this game, your Innkeeper

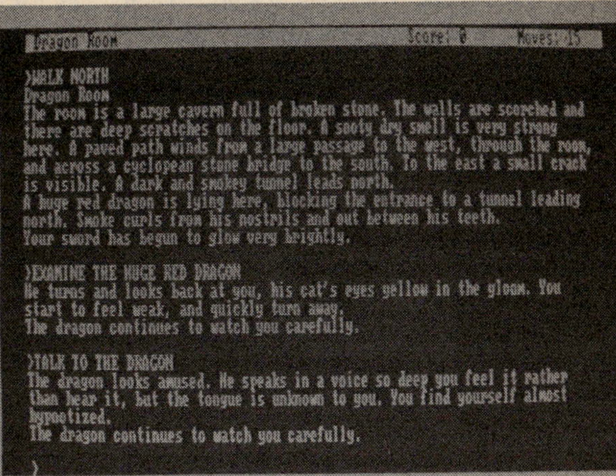

Figure 2.6   Zork II

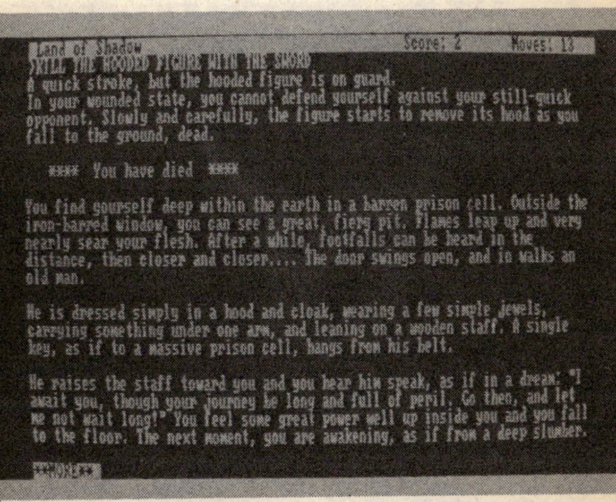

Figure 2.7   Zork III

sells you what you need. You begin with a specific number of silver coins. You are told how many coins you have and are given numbers signifying intelligence, intuition, ego, strength, constitution, and dexterity. This is important information if you are to spend your silver coins wisely.

After you name your character, the innkeeper asks, *Wilt thou buy one of our fine swords*? If you answer yes, you are presented with a menu of available swords, complete with prices. There is quite a range. You can get anything from a dagger to a great sword. After you make a selection, the bargaining starts. When you reach a price agreeable to you both, the innkeeper asks if you would like to purchase a shield. The game proceeds in like manner as you bargain for armor, a bow, arrows, and salve for wounds.

You then select the level of difficulty, and play begins. The display pictures you moving through rooms in a labyrinth filled with treasures, traps, and monsters. The unique thing about

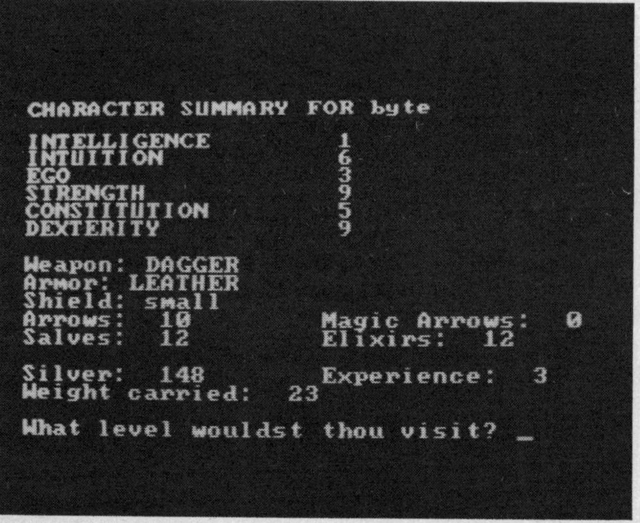

**Figure 2.8   Temple of Apshai: you begin
by equipping your character for battle.**

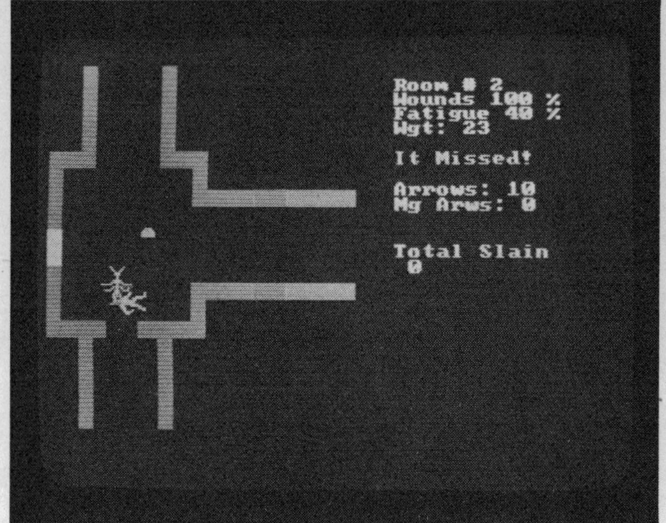

Figure 2.9   Temple of Apshai

this game is that the battles you wage with the various monsters resemble action games. You move your character from room to room, attack, thrust, or parry with your sword, fire a normal arrow or a magic arrow, or change weapons. You must be careful not to move too quickly, for an attack by a monster while you are fatigued is deadly. You must contend with skeletons, zombies, spiders, wraiths, and more, as you attempt to accumulate treasure and escape unharmed.

This game is entertaining, especially for children. The graphics are sometimes more interesting for younger players than are text-only adventure games. *Temple of Apshai* is therefore a good introduction to adventure games for children ten years and older.

As we mentioned before, fantasy games have traditionally depended more on strategy and logic and less on fine muscle coordination and quick reactions. We suspect that future games will, like *Temple of Apshai*, merge some of the aspects of action games with fantasy games. Fantasy games will probably continue to appeal mostly to older children and adults, because of the logic required.

Epyx, the company that produced *Temple of Apshai* also sells several other adventure games for the IBM PC that use color graphics displays. One, *Star Warrior*, pits you, a lone space warrior, against all sorts of magical and ordinary perils as you fight against the Furies on the Planet Fornax. Another, *Crush, Crumble and Chomp!* is subtitled *The Movie Monster Game*. This one lets you control famous monsters from the movies while they destroy cities. If you've ever had the urge to send Godzilla against Washington, D.C., or The Glob against New York, this game may interest you.

Simulation Games

Simulation games are a special type of fantasy-adventure that give you a simulated experience like flying an airplane or

Figure 2.10   Star Warrior

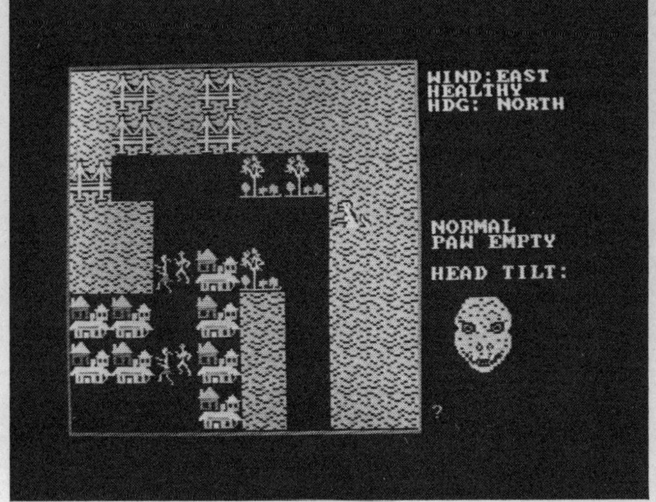

Figure 2.11   Crush, Crumble, and Chomp!

running a large corporation. Some computerized simulations actually do prepare people for the real experience, such as flight simulators used by the Air Force or NASA, while others are purely for fun.

Deadline

Deadline is a unique game from Infocom. Actually, we could have discussed this game in the fantasy-adventure category, but we really couldn't decide where to put it. It *is* an adventure, but in a sense it's also a simulation. It's a simulation of a detective's work, and it's really fun! A text-only game, it's head and shoulders above the early text-only games. What makes *Deadline* so much fun is the way it can understand so many different things you type in. This has become something of a trademark for Infocom.

Traditionally, text-only computer games for microcomputers have only been able to understand one or two-word com-

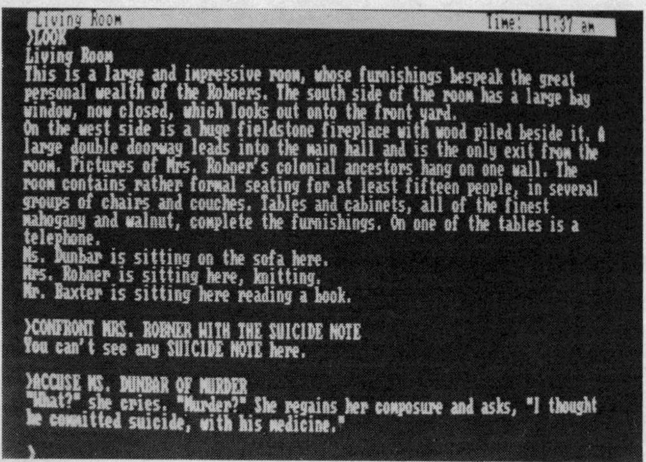

Figure 2.12   Deadline

mands. It can be terribly frustrating to ask the same question in as many different two-word combinations as you can think of, only to have the program continue to tell you it doesn't understand your question. In *Deadline*, you are not restricted to two-word commands but can type in things like "Put the knife in the trophy case," or "Unlock the door with the key," and the program understands perfectly. Of course you can't talk to this program as you would to a friend, but its ability to understand a variety of commands and sentence structures is truly amazing!

Deadline puts you in the role of a tough private eye out to solve the mystery of the death of Mr. Marshall Robner, millionaire industrialist and philanthropist. Robner was found dead on the floor of his library, the victim of an apparent overdose of the tranquilizer he had been taking. The door was locked from the inside. Robner had experienced recent business setbacks and had been suffering from severe bouts of depression. It seems to be an open-and-shut case of suicide. But is it? It's up to you to find out.

You are a private detective. You have been hired by Robner's attorney to investigate this presumed suicide. The attorney is convinced there was no foul play, but he feels an investigation is in order since Robner was in the process of changing his will when he died. Mrs. Robner is reluctant to cooperate, but grudgingly agrees to let you spend one day in the Robner mansion to investigate the death. Therefore, you have twelve hours to complete your investigation and solve the case.

Each turn consumes one minute of time. A line at the top of the screen tells you how much time you have left. You are

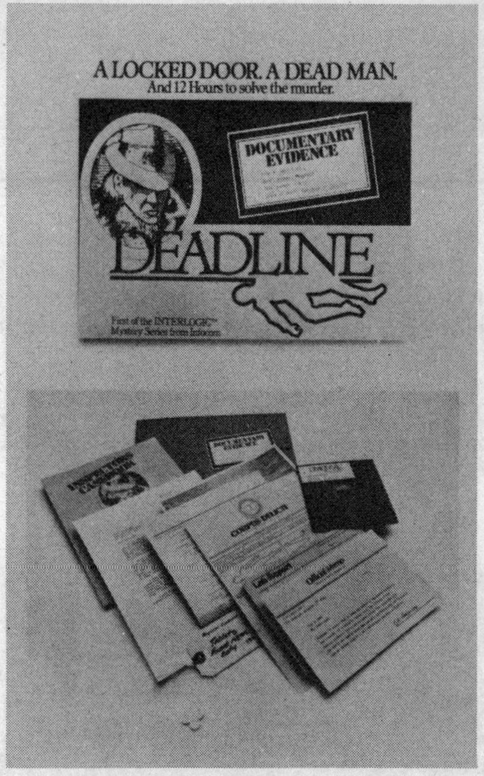

Figure 2.13   Deadline packaging

free to move around the Robner mansion and examine anything or anybody you please.

At first, the people you meet seem ordinary enough, but are they? There's Mrs. Robner, who was frequently visited by gentlemen callers and who is obviously NOT grief stricken over her husband's death. Then there is Ms. Dunbar, Robner's personal secretary, who seems to have been unusually close to Robner. And then there is George, the spoiled son who often quarrelled with his father. You wonder too about Mr. Baxter, Robner's business partner, who may have more to gain from Robner's death than anyone suspects. There is also Mrs. Rourke, the housekeeper, who seems innocent enough, but who takes an unnatural interest in the personal affairs of everyone in the Robner household. There are other characters as well. You are free to wander the estate, examine, question, fingerprint and analyze to your heart's content. Meanwhile, the clock ticks on.

This is an elegant game, beautifully and artfully packaged. It comes complete with a letter of employment from Robner's attorney, a coroner's report, a photo of the death scene, a crime lab analysis of the teacup, a police report, a transcript of interviews with all the people concerned with the case, and even three of the "deadly pills" found near the body. A fine manual explains how to play the game and how to talk to the program in language it will understand.

It will take most people about twenty hours to complete this game. You can save it at any point and resume it later. Anyone who enjoys mysteries will love this Infocom game. It sets a new standard for text-only games. This one's a winner.

Suspended

This is another excellent simulation from Infocom (diskette—$49.95). As with *Deadline*, the packaging is excellent. The game comes with a heavy playing board to help you keep track of what's going on.

The plot is a science fiction simulation. You were chosen by lottery to be placed in suspended animation. Your mind is used to control the life systems of an entire planet. This should have continued for 500 years. As the game begins, you have been unexpectedly awakened to cope with an emergency. You must first determine what the emergency was, then deal with it.

You control six robots—Iris, Auda, Whiz, Waldo, Sensa, and Poet. Each of these robots has distinct strengths and weaknesses. Iris, for example, is highly visual but has limited mobility. Auda has unbelievably good hearing but is not equipped to carry out fine manipulations. You may address all of the robots at once or any one of them. Each will reply, and each seems to take on a personality as the game develops.

This is another first-rate game. Like *Deadline*, the program understands a sizable vocabulary of complex sentences. Both

Figure 2.14   Suspended packaging

games have been called *participatory novels*. That seemed a little outlandish before we really played these games. It doesn't anymore.

Avalon Hill Games

Avalon Hill is a major producer of adventure game-simulation programs. The company has a variety of well-designed games, many of which have a military theme. *VC*, for example, puts you in charge of a mission in Viet Nam in which your air cavalry, field artillery, and ARVN soldiers sweep through a section of the delta and try to clear the area of Viet Cong troops. Another program, *B-1 Nuclear Bomber*, lets you pilot a B-1 bomber that receives a top-priority coded message instructing you to prepare to drop a nuclear bomb on Moscow. We won't comment on our view of military games in general, but the games from Avalon Hill are well-done.

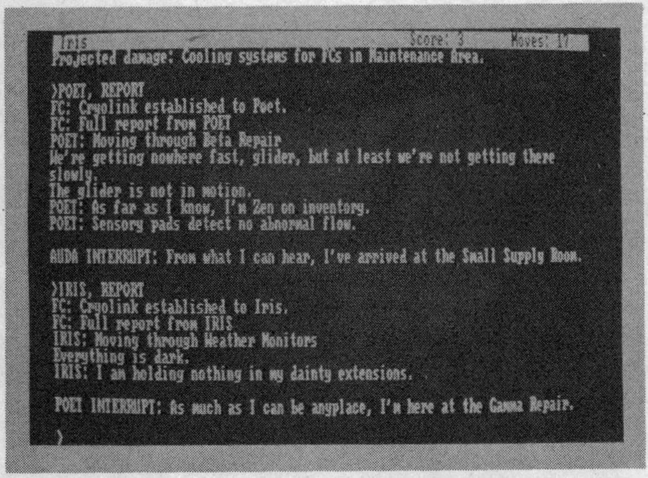

Figure 2.15   Suspended

Microsoft Flight Simulator

No section on simulations would be complete without at least one flying simulation. This one is probably the best of the bunch and is available for the IBM PC for $50 from Microsoft. You will need 64K of memory and a color/graphics adapter.

This simulation will not only entertain you; it will teach you some things about flying. The game features flight instruments displayed on half the screen. Airspeed indicator, artificial horizon, altimeter, turn-and-bank indicator, gyrocompass, and rate-of-climb indicator are included. So are an omni-bearing indicator, tachometer, and radio dials. A digital clock, magnetic compass, OLS marker indicators, fuel indicators, and oil and temperature gauges are also displayed. There are also indicators for instrument lights, carburetor, magneto, landing gear, flaps, elevators, trim, rudder, aileron, and throttle.

Eight windows are visible, and the realism of this color display is well-known among IBM PC owners. Sky, water, and clouds appear and are realistic. Five major cities have been programmed into this unbelievably good simulation. Seattle, Los Angeles, Chicago, Boston, and New York are all represented.

We aren't going to give many more details of this program. It is simply the best aircraft simulation we have seen. It could take you years to explore all the options it has. You can even elect to fly at night or engage in aerial combat. Aerobatic flying is another possibility.

In this sophisticated flight simulation, landings are realistic. You'll need practice to avoid catastrophe. This is definitely an adult program, and you can learn a lot about flying from it.

Millionaire

This sophisticated stock market simulation game is available from Blue Chip Software for $99.95. You will need 64K and

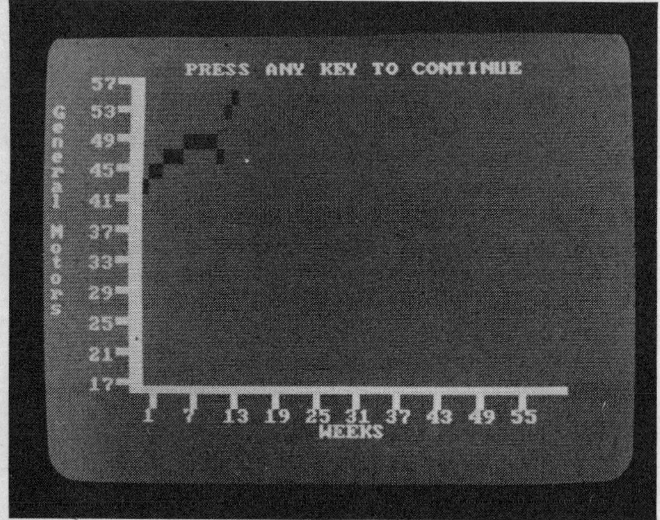

Figure 2.16   Millionaire

one disk drive. This adult game is too sophisticated for young children and takes one player. You are given complex market charts, tables showing highs and lows, world and national news items, and stock prices. With this information, you must decide when to buy and sell. The game is simple to learn and easy to play if you understand just a little about stocks.

Stock Market

Stock Market is a much simpler simulation of buying and selling stocks. You begin with $10,000 and try to run that up into a fortune. As many as 20 people can play this game, and it's a good way to learn some basic facts about investment. This text-only game sells for $10 and is published by Software Laboratories.

Oil Barons

Oil Barons is a sophisticated simulation of the oil business. It lets from one to eight players try their luck at obtaining oil leases, drilling for oil, and running an oil production company. This program, from Epyx, is one of the better simulations of its type and has good color graphics. It comes with a large color game board and playing pieces that show you where your leases and wells are.

Card Games, Las Vegas-Style Games, and Board Games

Championship Blackjack

In *Championship Blackjack* you play against the casino. This program from PC Software sells for $34.95. There are many options to choose from, including the ability to use rules followed by casinos in different parts of the world. You can get suggestions for what you ought to do at any time. You can also use the program to learn Julian Braun's point-counting system for estimating odds. This is a good program for beginners just learning the game, or for experts who are honing their skills.

Bridge Tutor

Unlike *Championship Blackjack*, *Bridge Tutor* helps you learn to play the game. This program sells for $60 and is for those who are serious about learning the fine points of the game. Bridge isn't a simple game, and no computer program can make it really easy to learn. *Bridge Tutor* is an aid, but you'll still have to work at learning.

Hi-Roller Casino

This package has several attractive features. First, it will run on an IBM PC with a monochrome video card. It does not

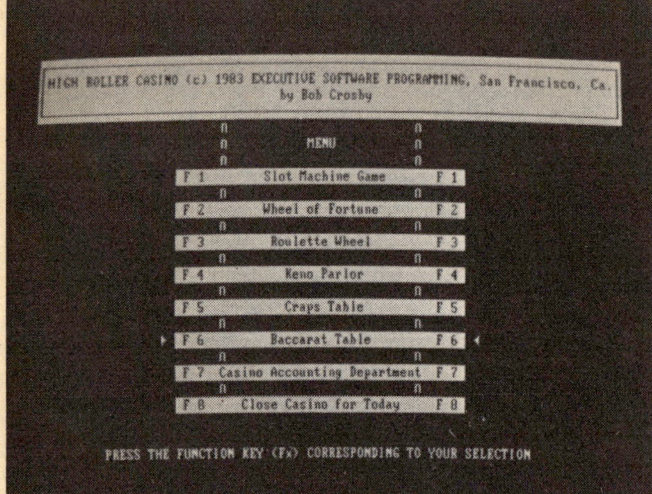

Figure 2.17   Hi-Roller Casino: main menu

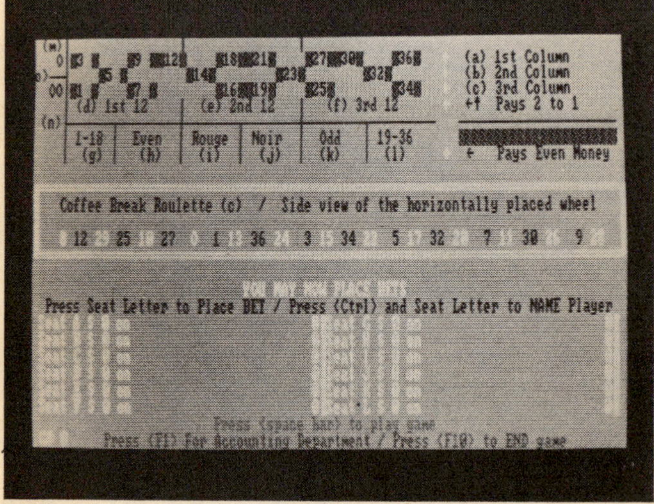

Figure 2.18   Hi-Roller Casino: Roulette

require a color/graphics card. Second, *Hi-Roller Casino* consists of a whole set of games. You get good versions of Slot Machine, Wheel of Fortune, Roulette, Keno, Baccarat and Craps. All the programs simulate the real thing and use standard "American" casino gaming rules. The program keeps track of your winnings (or losses) and can handle several players. *Hi-Roller Casino* is available from Executive Software Programming for $49.95.

Hi-Rollers

Hi-Rollers really has four games: *Slots*, *Craps*, *Roulette*, and *Blackjack*. The program sells for $47 and requires 48K and the color/graphics adapter. It is published by New Venture Systems. These games are fun for the whole family.

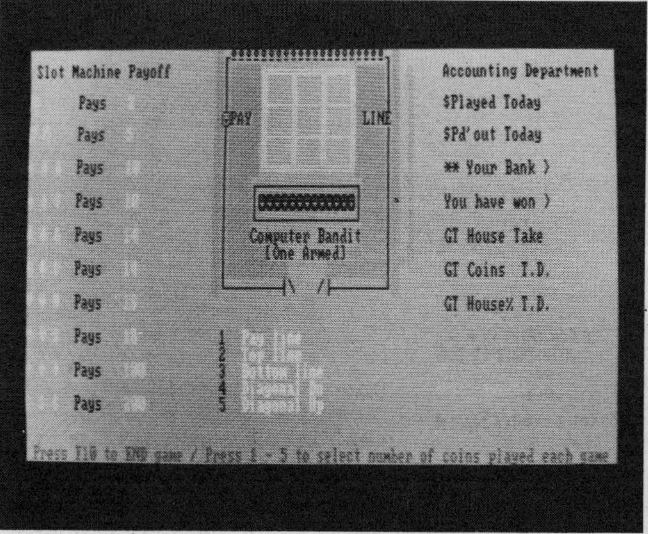

Figure 2.19   Hi-Roller Casino: Slot Machine

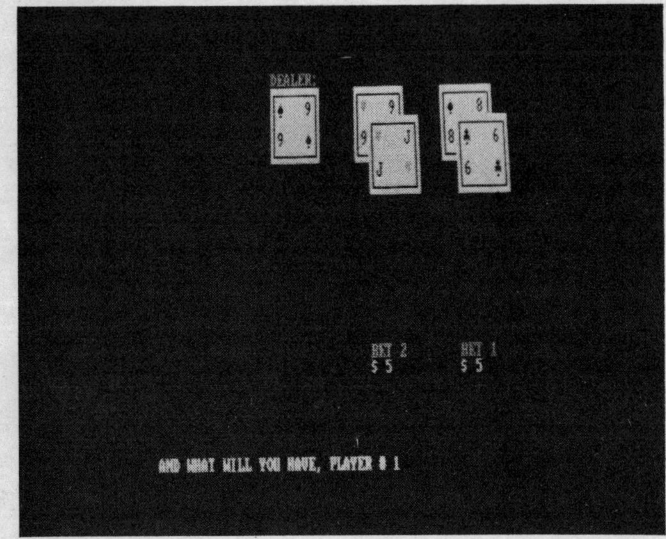

Figure 2.20   Fun 10: Blackjack

Board Games

Backgammon/Checkers

These programs sell for $39.95 each and are designed to give you an opponent or keep track of the game if you play a friend. You'll need 64K for either of these games from Comprehensive Software Support.

Fun 10

Here is an inexpensive way ($29.95) to introduce your family to game-playing on the PC. This disk has ten games, including Cribbage and Othello. Also included are some maze and arcade-type games. The package is published by Ensign Software. You need only 48K and the color/graphics adapter for this series of interesting game programs.

Galaxy

This board game is similar to the Parker Brothers board game called *Risk*. The difference is the setting. Up to twenty players try to acquire and exploit up to forty planets. This is not a graphics game. You don't need color, and only 48K are necessary to play this Avalon Hills game that sells for $25.

Call to Arms

Call to Arms bears a much greater resemblance to *Risk*. In fact, it is nothing more than a computerized version of that game. The object of this game is to conquer the world. The game is played on a map of 36 European countries with from one to five players. This game has had wide appeal in the non-electronic version. List price is $29.95 from Sirius Software.

Sports Games

There are many sports games available for your IBM computer. Many are suitable for both children and adults, but they do presuppose a knowledge of the rules of each game.

Hi-Res Computer Golf

This highly acclaimed Avant-Garde Creations sports program surprised a lot of people and became an almost instant best-seller. Up to four players can play at one time. There are five eighteen-hole courses to play on. The timing of your swing is the key in this game, and you need a game paddle to play. The course has sand traps and all the other trappings (no pun intended). This $34.95 game is really fun.

Decathlon

Decathlon became an overnight classic for the Apple computer. Microsoft has recently produced a version for the IBM requiring 64K and color/graphics adapter and monitor. The game sells for $35 and promises to be as big a success as the Apple version.

One to six players can play this graphic recreation of the ten-event Olympic competition. The graphics are absolutely great in this version. You use the keyboard to manipulate the contestants. Music and sound effects are included.

Before the real competition begins, you can practice each event to your heart's content. The competition includes the 100-meter dash, the high jump, the javelin, and other Olympic Decathlon events.

Pro Football

This is an entirely different kind of sports program intended for the serious gambler. *Pro Football* from Computer Sports Systems handicaps pro games against the Las Vegas betting line. This isn't a game, and it obviously isn't for children. Neither is the price, since *Pro Football* sells for $195!

Other Sports Programs

There are many sports programs available for your IBM. Avalon Hill Microcomputer Games sells some good ones. *Computer Football Strategy* is one of the best computer football games we have played. This game was developed with help from *Sports Illustrated Magazine* and sells for $30.

The football field is displayed, and you are asked what you want to run. If you don't have a human opponent, you can choose to play the computer. After you enter your choices, the computer runs the play. A small arrow on the field shows the movement of the ball, and the computer displays statistics such as down, yardline, and so on.

CHAPTER THREE

Arts And Crafts

If you have ever watched an excellent video game running on a personal computer like the IBM PC, you were probably impressed by two things: the quality of the color graphics and animation and the sound effects. The PC has the ability to create outstanding color graphics, and it has a built-in sound synthesizer as well. We'll introduce you to these two features and explain how they can be used for recreational computing and for business applications.

HOW TO USE YOUR IBM PERSONAL COMPUTER FOR ARTS AND CRAFTS

We won't tell you that after a weekend of study, you will be able to replace your baby grand piano or electric organ with the PC. You won't be able to press a button and get a Picasso to hang on your wall. It probably won't take the place of music or art lessons either, but there are many creative and enjoyable things you can do.

If you are just getting acquainted with computers, you probably won't be able to create a video game that sells millions of copies. That takes a considerable amount of knowledge about how computers operate, as well as some creative and artistic genius most of us just don't have. However, many of the creators of video games began by buying a computer and

**Figure 3.1   Children enjoy using an
IBM Personal Computer at home.**

learning how it operates. They didn't necessarily have formal training or college degrees in computer science or engineering. If you are skilled in creating color pictures and animated drawings on the computer screen, you can put these skills to work by adding interest and excitement to game and educational programs. You might also create music on the IBM PC and add it to software.

Creating video games is not the only way to take advantage of the PC's video and sound features. Serious artists and musicians are now using personal computers in their work. High-quality art and music is now possible on small computers like the IBM PC. Many businesses also use the PC to create charts and graphs, which are converted to printed illustrations for reports and to figures that can be displayed on an overhead projector at meetings. Artistic, business, and recreational applications of sound and graphics will be discussed in this chapter.

The Unadorned IBM PC

Your IBM PC is potentially a powerful graphics and sound machine. We say potential, because when you turn on the computer and load the first program into its memory, all you are likely to see on the screen are letters and numbers made up of little dots on the computer screen. As you run a typical program, the only sound the computer is likely to produce is an occasional beep. You may be thinking that a picture made up of dots on the screen can't really be that good. And when you hear the computer make its first beep, it will be hard to believe that it can make music. Remember that the image on a regular television program is really a pattern of dots. Television displays are made up of even more individual dots than the IBM PC can control, but the principle is still the same. When we look at a bunch of dots, our mind does its best to see them as a meaningful whole, as a picture. When you get all the dots arranged in just the right way, you get a nice colored picture. A similar thing takes place with sound. Music is nothing more than sound that is carefully organized. If you have control over sound so that you can make it higher or lower, louder or softer, longer or shorter, you can at least create some simple and pleasing musical compositions. By building on these basic principles, you can turn the PC into a powerful artistic and musical tool.

The PC is one of the best graphics computers on the market today. Because it is so good, it is complicated to understand. While most business and professional computers have limited graphics, usually black and white, the PC can generate many types of graphics and is available in two versions, a *monochrome display* model and a *color/graphics* model. The monochrome display creates ordinary text on the screen of your video monitor, while the color/graphics version can display text and several types of color graphics. We will focus on the color/graphics version in this chapter.

IBM PC graphics can be complex, but the principle is simple. Regular text is displayed on the screen by dividing the screen up into 25 lines of 80 squares. The computer can individually control what is displayed in each of those 80 squares on each line. Thus, there are 2000 different locations on the screen where the computer can display a character. The letters, numbers, and symbols displayed in those 2000 locations are formed on the screen by lighting up tiny dots. If you watch the scoreboard at a football or basketball game you probably noticed that each location where a number can be displayed on the scoreboard is a square or rectangle filled with small lights. Each number is made by turning on some of the lights. One pattern forms a 2, another pattern forms a 9, and so on. Computer displays work the same way. They have more squares than the scoreboard, and the dots are smaller, but computers display an A, a B, or any other character on the screen by displaying a pattern of tiny dots. This is called a *dot matrix* display. Dot matrix printers create characters on paper in the same way.

Think of the computer screen as a square divided into many smaller squares. When the PC is turned on it automatically goes to its text mode display format. That is, it prepares to work with 25 lines of 80 squares on the screen. If you press the C key, the computer will display that letter in the square where the cursor is located. Pressing the C determined which of the dots of light in the square would be on and which would be off. Thus, pressing C might turn on fifteen or twenty dots of light in that square so the shape of the C is displayed. Text mode displays let you control lots of dots with one keypress. In addition to letters, numbers, and regular symbols, the IBM PC even has a few special symbols, such as a tiny smiling face and the symbols for heart, club, spade, and diamond. They can be displayed in a screen location just like regular letters and numbers. When you use these special symbols that are the same size as ordinary characters, you are using *low-resolution graphics*. With low-resolution graphics on the IBM PC, you control 2000 display squares on the screen (25 lines of 80 characters). This method of generating graphics is the one you would use if you have the monochrome display card. If you have the color/graphics card, you can control the color of the character, the background color, and the color of the border around the low-resolution or text display. That is only the beginning of the types of graphics you can display with a color/ graphics card.

In low-resolution graphics you are limited to 2000 rather large display elements. You can create some interesting pictures, but they will look a bit crude because each element is so large. It is a little like drawing with a large, blunt crayon. The PC with a color/graphics card gives you two color graphics modes: a *medium-resolution* mode and the *high-resolution* mode. Both let you create graphics displays consisting of many more small dots or elements of color.

In the medium-resolution mode, the screen is divided into 200 rows, and each row can display 320 dots of light. That gives you control over 64,000 little dots on the screen. You can determine whether each of these dots is on or off, and you can turn them on in any of sixteen different colors. Each dot, by the way, is called a *picture element* or *pixel*. By controlling which of the pixels is on and what colors they display, you can create some sophisticated graphics.

For even greater detail, you can use the high-resolution graphics mode. In it the computer displays 200 rows of 640 dots. That gives you control over 128,000 pixels! Using high-resolution graphics can limit you to only one color, but you can get some very detailed displays.

THE SOUND OF MUSIC
ON THE IBM PC

The unadorned IBM PC has a built-in circuit called a *sound generator* or *sound synthesizer*. It is this sound generator that makes the beep when you turn on the computer. By controlling the sound generator, you can tell the computer to generate sound effects and music. The BASIC that comes with the PC has several keywords that make it easier to write programs to generate sound and music.

Some Music Principles

Before we discuss the way the IBM PC generates sound, we will give you an overview of some important *music jargon* (and you thought only computers had jargon):

• *Pitch* is determined by the frequency (cycles per second) of the sound. We hear cycles or waves created by vibrations in the air. These are measured in cycles per second, or Hertz. You can hear sounds between 20 and 15,000 Hertz. Notes on a piano or any other musical instrument are organized by pitch. The notes created by a piano are organized into several *octaves*. A piano has slightly more than an eight-octave range, from deep or bass sounds to high-pitched notes. An octave is a group of sounds, not a single sound. An octave might begin with the C note and progress up through notes D, E, F, G, A, and B. The next C note ends that octave and begins the next highest octave. Composers and musicians have created a complicated system of naming sounds of different pitch and duration, but the primary difference between one note on a piano and another is the pitch (the Hertz of the sound).

• *Amplitude* or *loudness* of the sound. We experience this as variations in the volume of the sound.

• *Duration* is the amount of time the sound is made. There are symbols and notation conventions that tell the musician exactly how much time to play each note in a composition.

• The *envelope* of the sound is the variation of loudness over the period it is heard. Different sounds have different *attack* and *decay* patterns. Some reach their maximum loudness gradually and then trail off. Others begin at maximum amplitude and stop abruptly. The pattern of changes in amplitude of a tone help determine the timbre.

• *Timbre* is the musician's term for the complexity of sound. Some sounds are pure tones; they have only one pitch. Others have a major tone and many harmonic or secondary frequencies that add richness to the sound. These secondary sounds are part of what gives each musical instrument its own personality.

Programming Your Own Music

One way to get your IBM PC to make music is to learn a computer language. Since the IBM PC has a sound generator built in, you can use keywords in the IBM versions of the various computer languages to generate sound and music. Several programming languages can be used, and each has a way of telling the computer to make sounds. The most commonly used computer language is BASIC. In BASICA, you can use the keyword SOUND to tell the computer to make a sound. SOUND must be followed by two numbers: the first number tells the computer the frequency or pitch of the sound, and the second number tells the computer the duration of the sound. SOUND 523.25, 18.2 tells the computer to make a C note (523.25 cycles per second) and hold it for one second. Duration is measured by a timing device inside the computer called a clock; 18.2 ticks of the clock is equal to one second. The SOUND keyword will generate sounds with a pitch between 37 and 32,767 Hertz, and the duration of the sound can be anything from a fraction of a second to over 60 minutes.

You cannot control the envelope or timbre with SOUND, but you can do some interesting work with sound and music with the PC. This simple BASIC instruction can be expanded to tell the computer to make notes with different pitches and durations. If you would like more information on programming music in BASIC, a well-stocked bookstore should have several books on the topic. In addition, the May 1983 issue of *PC World* carried an article titled "Programming Sound in BASIC." The article includes several programs you can type in to instruct the computer to play several musical numbers.

In addition to the SOUND keyword, BASICA has another important word for music generation. PLAY lets you give the computer instructions in a format similar to standard musical notation. With PLAY you can define the octave to be used and then specify the notes in letters from A to G. PLAY lets you generate notes across a seven-octave range.

There is a program with the do-it-yourself approach. If you don't know a programming language like BASIC, you can't get the computer to make sounds. Learning a programming language just to tell your computer to make sounds isn't worth it to many people. Even if you do know BASIC or some other language, programming music into the computer can be a slow job. There is a solution to this dilemna: you can use software and extra pieces of hardware.

SOFTWARE AND PERIPHERALS FOR MUSIC

Many popular computers, including the IBM PC, can run music composer programs that make writing and playing music and sound effects much easier than it is when you have only the keywords in BASIC.

At present, there isn't much music software available for the IBM PC. While such programs abound for other personal computers like the Apple II and ATARI, we were only able to locate one for the IBM PC. We think this is because the IBM is viewed primarily as a business computer. It is only now beginning to be used for such things as video games and home applications. Since there are no obstacles to using the IBM PC for music and in fact some advantages, this software will probably begin to appear soon.

The Keyboard piano

This program from Europro converts the IBM PC into a piano keyboard. This is slightly misleading since the software obviously doesn't change the IBM keyboard at all. What it does is change the signal sent to the computer from the keyboard. Ordinarily when you press the letter A on the keyboard, the keyboard tells the computer to print the letter A on the screen. With *The Keyboard Piano* software, when you press the letter A, the keyboard tells the computer to sound a musical tone. When you press other letters, the computer sounds other tones. A template displayed on the screen tells you what keys represent the various musical notes.

The Keyboard Piano won't turn your IBM PC into a $4000 electronic piano. Since it uses no additional hardware to generate more complex sound beyond what the sound generator inside the computer can produce, the richness of the tones and the complexity of the musical numbers are limited. But it should give you an entertaining way to use your IBM PC. To use this software package, you need at least 64K of memory, one disk drive unit, and a color/graphics card. It is well worth its price of $50.

Music Training

Some software packages use the music capabilities of the computer to put it in the role of a music teacher. Programs that use the computer to teach music are generally drill and practice programs. That is, they do things like sound a note and have the student name the note. Or they play a short melody and then have the student program the same melody back into the computer.

EDUMUSIC I

This program is intended to teach music theory to beginning musicians of all ages. It presents a thorough step-by-step method of learning the following musical principles:

* Rhythm
* Music symbols
* Melody and chords

Graphic representations of musical notes and note patterns are shown on the screen as the notes are sounded. Basic instructions, questions and answer sessions, and drill and practice sessions are all part of the training. *The Keyboard Piano* program is also included in this package. It is *The Keyboard Piano* program that lets you respond to those parts of a training session where musical notes are required.

This package includes three diskettes and a ten-page instruction booklet. To use this system, you need an IBM PC with 64K memory, one disk drive, and a color/graphics card. EDUMUSIC is available from Europro, Inc., and sells for $80.

EDUMUSIC II

This software package, also sold by Europro is an extension of *EDUMUSIC I*. Designed for more advanced learners, it follows a format similar to EDUMUSIC I but goes into higher levels of music theory training. This program's musical training can be applied to many different musical instruments. The price for this package is also $80.

VISUAL ARTS AND THE IBM PC

Can you really be an artist with the IBM PC? The question of art is a tricky one and subject to much snobbery. But with the IBM PC, you can create some interesting and attractive visual designs using its graphics capabilities. One person who is definitely convinced that computer art is real art is Mark Wilson. *PC Magazine* covers Wilson's art work and some of his ideas on computer art in the April 1983 issue. Wilson has had several one-man art shows in New York and now makes his living doing art on his IBM PC, with a color monitor and a color printer. Wilson believes that computers, although they are still in their infancy, will be important artistic tools in the future.

The most straightforward and cheapest way to get started in graphics, of course, is to program the computer yourself. With the IBM PC or any other computer, you can create a variety of patterns on the screen by using simple commands. Just as with music, the computer can only do what it is capable of understanding and in its own language. You tell it what to do in a programming language like BASIC. The BASIC that comes with the disk version of the IBM PC is well-endowed with keywords for color graphics. They keyword LINE lets you create lines of varying lengths on the screen; CIRCLE is a simple way of creating circles, ellipses, and arcs in any of several colors; and PAINT lets you fill in areas of the screen with a color. An IBM PC with disk drives runs a BASIC with some of the best and easiest-to-use graphics instructions currently available. Several books on creating color graphics in IBM versions of BASIC should be available by the time you read this.

As with music, the creation of graphics in BASIC can be tedious. Fortunately, there are many programs that make the job of creating graphics much easier.

Graphics Software

Several programs are available that translate your simple instructions into codes the computer understands. For example, in many graphics software packages, you simply move the cursor around on the screen by pressing the arrow keys on the keyboard or by using a joystick. As the cursor moves, it leaves a line in much the same way Etch-A-Sketch creates lines on its screen. With some practice, you can draw intricate designs.

Glyphix

This graphics software is an inexpensive general system. Sold by Starside Engineering, it costs only $24.95. To use the software effectively, you need another program called *Frieze* sold by the same company for $55. *Frieze* prints the graphics displays you create with *Glyphix*.

With *Glyphix*, you can think of the screen as a new drawing pad and the cursor as the point of a pencil. Now think of the back-space key as an eraser, and you have an idea of how *Glyphix* works. You can move the cursor around on the screen by pressing keys on the numberpad.The 4, 8, 6, and 2 keys all have arrows on them.The cursor moves in the direction of the arrow when one of these keys is pressed. The 1, 7, 9, and 3 keys on the numberpad move the cursor in diagonal directions. This program lets you draw rough, lower-resolution graphics or finer, more detailed graphics by adjusting the size of the pixels the program uses. This is done by pressing the Z key and then typing a number from 1 to 50. When you are in the first degree (No. 1), curved lines will look rough. When you are in the fiftieth degree (No. 50), you can make smooth curves and circles. *Glyphix* can also make geometric shapes in several sizes. If you press the E key and follow it with numbers describing the size and shape, the program automatically draws circles, arcs, and pie segments.

The Graphic Solution

This software package does most of what *Glyphix* does and much more. Of course, it also costs more. Sold by Accent Software, the program costs $149.95. *The Graphics Solution* is truly designed for the computer artist. It has two basic creative features: drawing shapes and making them move. The main thing you can do with this package that you couldn't do with *Glyphix* is develop animated drawings and incorporate printed words. As an example, you can create a little cartoon with a man walking across the screen, his words appearing as he walks and talks. The animation is done by making a series of pictures of the man. These pictures are called frames, just as in the movies. *The Graphics Solution* keeps track of these frames and sequences them in a program that makes the final animated presentation. The program makes the job of developing animated sequences many times easier than it would be if you were doing it with a programming language like BASIC.

PC-Draw

This graphics software is aimed at the professional user, primarily the draftsmen and engineer. It is sold by Micrografx for $250. The most unique feature of this software is that one keypress can change a drawing. You can rotate the drawing, make it larger or smaller, and change the colors. The advantage of this feature is that you can look at your drawing from many different perspectives by pressing a series of keys. When you are finally satisfied with the size, shape, and color, you can save or print it out. You can name and number the pages of a printout just as you do in word processing. You divide a large drawing up into individual pages and label each page so that the total picture can easily be reassembled.

Peachtree Graphics Language

This program, which costs $395, is a sophisticated professional system that helps you create, display, and print detailed color graphics. The *Peachtree Graphics Language* is probably more difficult to learn to use than the instructions in BASIC. Its appeal then is not its simplicity but its sophistication. The program is really a comprehensive language with over 100 keywords, all of which will help you create color graphics. BAR, for example, lets you tell the computer to generate a bar of color. Numbers you provide tell the computer how long, how wide, and what color the bar should be. Other shapes can be created with keywords like CIRCLE, ARC, LINE, PIE, and RECTANGLE. You can also display several types of text

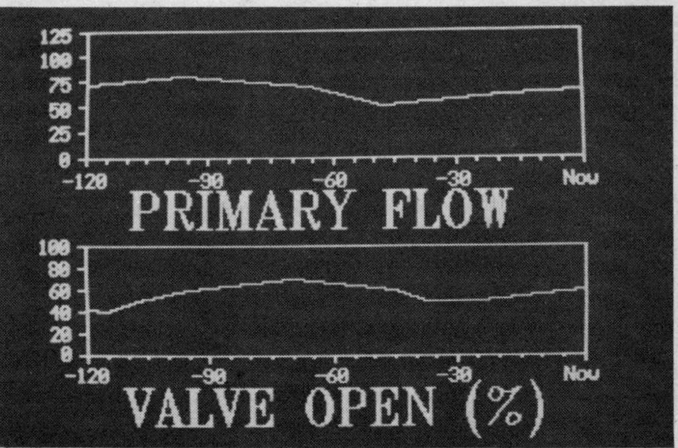

Figure 3.2   Peachtree Graphics Language
helps create, display, and print graphics.

in your graphics. For example, CHAR SLANT, lets you put slanted characters in the picture. You add a number to the instruction that tells the computer how much of a slant you want. The size of the characters can also be controlled by a simple command.

This program will be of most use to individuals who must regularly create graphs for business or professions. You can create a wide variety of graphics with this program: line drawings, bar charts and graphs, and *real time displays*, such as a strip chart in which the data changes as you watch it. There is even a ZOOM command that lets you enlarge a particular section of the graphic you have created. Peachtree includes a detailed weather map of the U.S. with fronts and rain clouds, created with *Peachtree Graphics Language*.

This program can display your creations in brilliant color on a color monitor connected to the IBM PC, but it can also send graphs, figures, and illustrations to special devices called

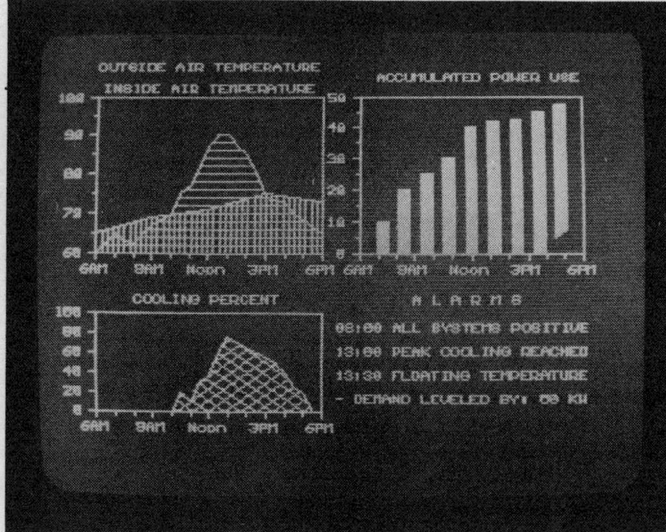

Figure 3.3   Peachtree Graphics Language
lets you display text in your graphics.

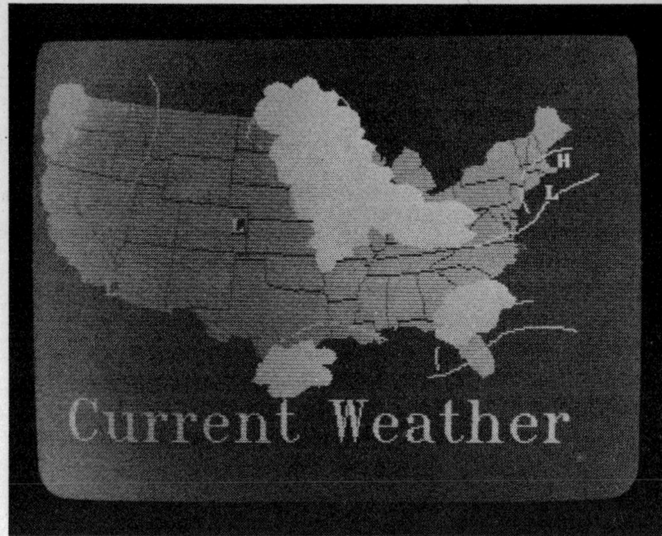

Figure 3.4   Created with Peachtree Graphics Language

plotters. A plotter will duplicate the screen illustration on paper or on a sheet of plastic (for overheads). The program works with Hewlett-Packard plotters. It can also send graphics (but not the color) to several models of printers made by Epson (the company that makes the dot matrix printer sold by IBM).

If you would like more information on programs like *Peachtree Graphics Language* you may want to read an article called "Business Graphics" by Ron Forbes in the October, 1983 issue of *Business Software*.

Business Graphics System

This is another program from Peachtree. It sells for $295. As the name implies, it's really designed for use in a business environment. It lets you create, with very little effort, a variety of business figures. Data you enter can be used to generate line and bar graphs, single-sided bar charts, double-sided bar charts, pie charts, histograms, and scatter charts. The program's ease of use means you are essentially limited to the basic chart and graph designs built into the program, but since ninety-five percent of the graphics used in business are of the types this program can create, that is generally not a problem. Output can be sent to monitors, printers, or plotters.

Special Input and Output
Devices for Graphics

Much of what you want to do with graphics, you can do with a good graphics software package and a dot matrix printer that can print graphics. The output from an ordinary printer like the Epson FX-80 is good but not great. If your interest in graphics is a professional one, you may be interested in some of the special devices designed just for graphics.

Special devices for getting graphics information into the computer are called digitizers or graphics tablets, and special

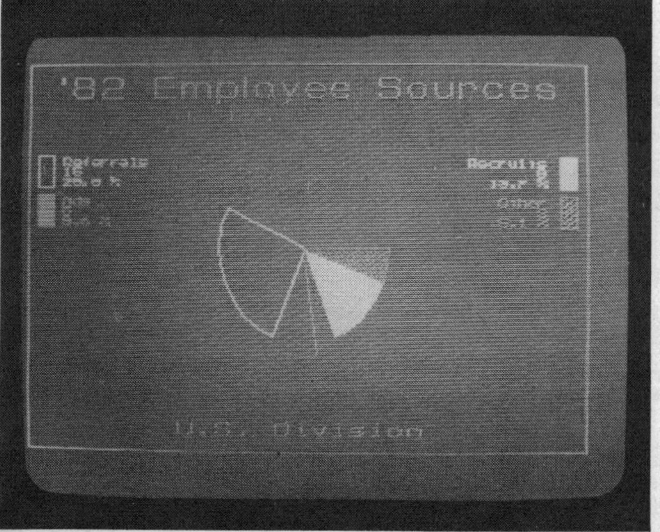

Figure 3.5   A pie chart using the Business Graphics System

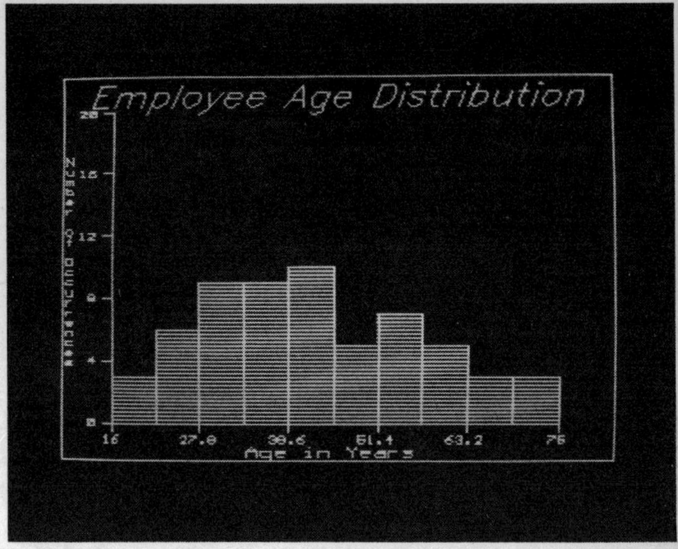

**Figure 3.6   A histogram created
with the Business Graphics System**

graphic output devices are called plotters or printer/plotters. All of these can be used only when you have the correct software.

A plotter is used to draw figures and graphs under the direction of a computer. Most plotters use different colored pens to draw designs. Houston Instruments, Comrex, Panasonic, Mannesman Talley, Hewlett Packard, and Strobe all sell plotters for personal computers like the IBM PC. Prices range from around $500 to several thousand dollars.

Plotters can create bar graphs, figures, and illustrations on paper or acetate sheets. The acetate sheets can be used with overhead projectors. Some PC owners are involved enough in graphics to justify buying a plotter, and many small businesses and colleges use them because they produce graphs and figures at a lower cost than those produced commercially.

Many models create graphs by moving pens on a flat surface. We used a different type, the drum plotter sold by Strobe.

This is a popular accessory because it is relatively inexpensive, yet lets you create sophisticated graphics. It uses a rotating drum where the paper or acetate sheet is placed to create the graphics. Strobe's three models sell for from $595 to $995.

Another company, Amdek, better known for its color video monitors, recently announced a complete business graphics system that costs $1995. Before you dismiss this product as too expensive we should mention that the price includes an Amdek color monitor, a well-designed plotter, a special interface card, and the BPS Business Graphics software system.

In addition to output devices such as plotters, you can also buy several devices for graphics data input. One type is called a graphics tablet or digitizer pad; it can be used to create figures, graphs, and tables on the screen of the computer. The tablet is generally a special pad about two feet square. You move a special stylus or sensor over its surface. As you move the stylus, a corresponding line is drawn on the screen. For example, you can put a map on your tablet, trace its outline with your stylus, and thus reproduce the map on the computer screen. The video image created can be saved on a disk and used later

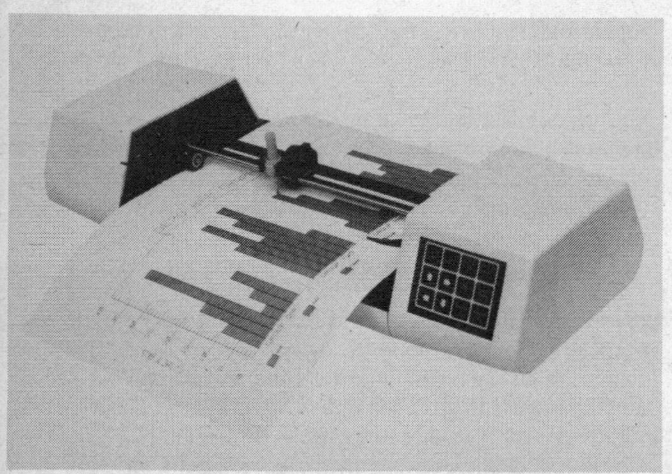

Figure 3.7   HIPLOT Plotter

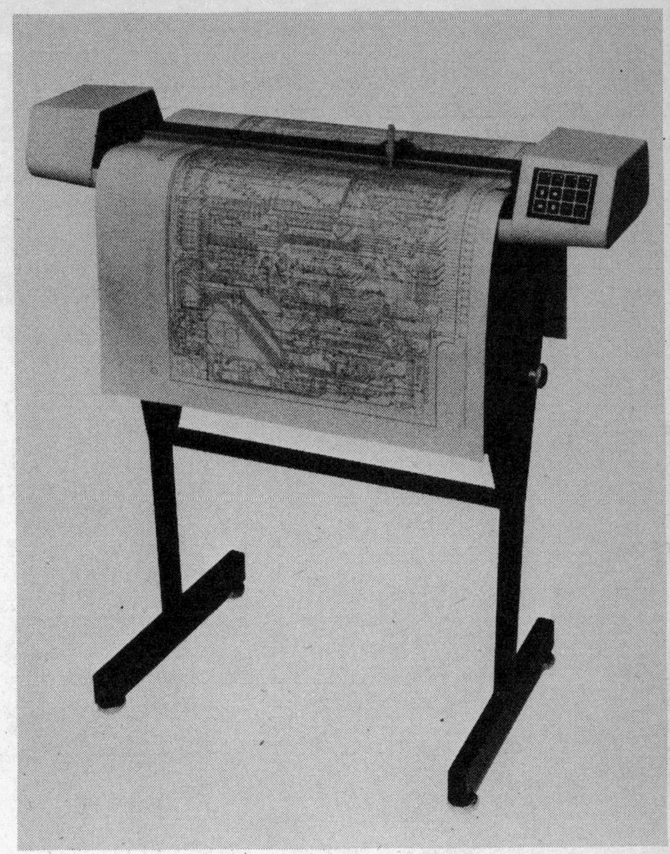

Figure 3.8   Houston Instruments Plotter

in a program. Graphics tablets vary in price but generally cost at least $200, usually more.

Houston Instruments sells a graphics tablet called *The HI-PAD Digitizer* which costs $895. Like most such devices, it can be used to create two-dimensional screen images. Several graphics tablets use the *pantograph* approach instead of a stylus to create designs. These have a hinged drawing arm that can be moved around on the surface of the tablet. As you move the arm, it sends data to the computer that creates a corresponding pattern on the screen of the computer. An inexpensive digitizer that uses the pantograph approach is the *VersaWriter*, which sells for $299. A $1700 pantograph system called the *Space Tablet Advanced Space Graphics System* lets you recreate three dimensional images on the screen. You can trace over the surface of an object such as an apple and see a three dimensional image of the apple created on your screen.

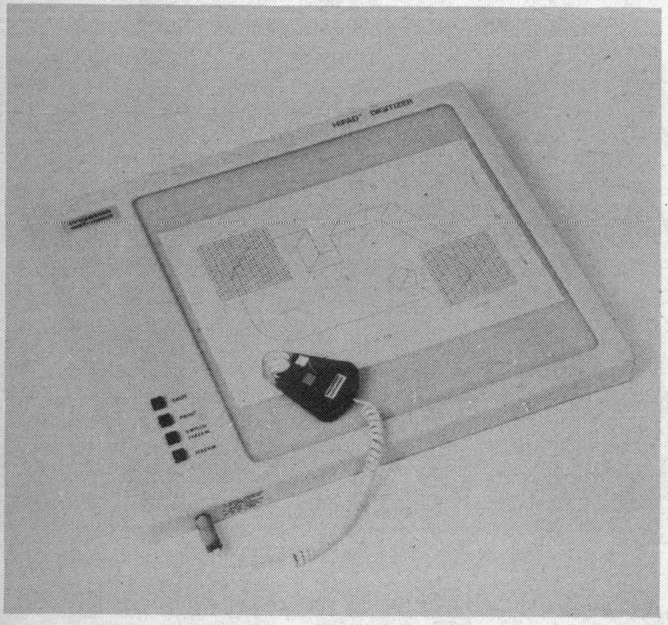

Figure 3.9   HIPAD Digitizer

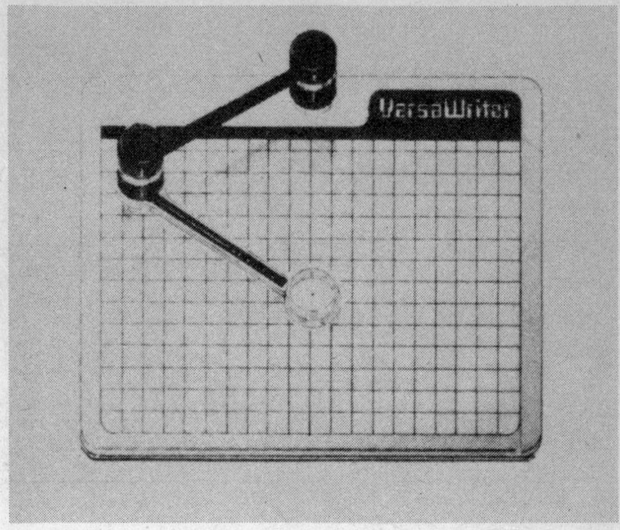

Figure 3.10   Versawriter

The IBM PC as Teacher

HOW COMPUTERS CAN HELP PEOPLE LEARN

Much is made of the ability of small computers like the IBM PC to function as educational devices in the home and classroom. However, the computer is only the latest in a long list of technological inventions that were supposed to revolutionize education in the twentieth century. In spite of the attention computers receive in the educational press, we do not believe they are likely to revolutionize the little red schoolhouse overnight. However, there is good reason to expect that education will evolve quickly in the coming years. There are two reasons for this: the decentralization of learning and the need for lifelong learning.

THE DESCHOOLING OF LEARNING

Education has been institutionalized for most of the twentieth century. Learning has been something children do in a classroom supervised by one or more adults. This model will continue to be important through the end of this century, but by the year 2000 it will play a smaller role than it does today. More people will spend time learning at home, in the office, at the factory, and at adult learning centers. Learning will be a lifelong task rather than something children do to prepare for adulthood.

In earlier times, you could learn a trade or profession and

then earn your livelihood for the rest of your life with those skills. Today virtually every job is being changed or eliminated by new information, new social trends, or new technology. Physicians, for example, cannot continue to practice medicine without keeping up with new discoveries that effect the way they practice. Other jobs disappear and are replaced by new ones. Like the wagon wheel factory that converts to hubcaps, many of us will have to learn a different profession or trade at least once in our lifetime. Most of us will find ourselves learning throughout our lives to keep up with change. Many of us will return to some sort of adult training program to retool for a new profession.

Even if your job stays stable, there are many other aspects of your life that will change. Our federal income tax is a good example. Changes in federal income tax laws can mean thousands of dollars to families with modest incomes. Failure to keep up with these changes can be an expensive oversight.

We must continue to learn, regardless of our age, if we are to cope with the demands of life. And we will learn someplace other than public school classrooms. Fortunately, small computers like the IBM PC can be helpful in both traditional and non-traditional learning environments. For example, families will be able to buy computer programs that teach them about new income tax laws. There are numerous programs for the IBM PC that computerize record keeping and filling in income tax forms.

THE SMALL COMPUTER AS A TEACHING MACHINE

You may be aware that the IBM Personal Computer has not been a best-selling educational computer. Schools have tended to purchase less expensive machines, like the TRS-80 Model 4, the Apple IIe, or the Texas Instruments 99/4A. Consequently, there has not been an abundance of educational software for the IBM computer. Programmers simply concentrated their efforts on writing educational software for other machines.

This is beginning to change. Software companies are realizing that thousands of families have IBM PCs and are looking for good educational software. The machine may have been purchased mainly for business uses, but now many of those owners are looking around for software to help the whole family learn. Therefore, more and more educational software is being written for the IBM PC. There is already a reasonably good selection to choose from, and more is appearing almost daily.

There's good news and bad news about educational software. The good news is that more and more programs are becoming available. The bad news is that educational software is often not as good as it could be. One of the most common criticisms is that it fails to use good principles of teaching. This happens because good computer programmers usually know little or nothing about teaching. And people who know how children learn usually don't know how to write computer programs.

Some large companies who specialize in educational materials are just beginning to take an interest in developing software for the IBM. Science Research Associates is developing a line of software entitled *Education Series Program Package*. Developmental Learning Materials, Inc. (DLM), has just extended an excellent line of learning games to the IBM PC, and dilithium Press is developing a series of adult education packages. Other companies will probably follow suit. We hope this trend improves the quality of educational software in general and software for the IBM PC in particular.

As more educational software for the IBM becomes available, more schools are purchasing the PC. IBM has recently funded a 10,000-student field test of a new computer-assisted basic-skills program for the PC called *Writing to Read*. This is exactly the kind of research needed to help develop good educational software. It's good business for IBM, too, of course. If they can encourage educational software development, they can sell more computers to schools and to parents of school children.

There are many ways computers like the IBM PC can help

you and your children learn. Currently most students, from elementary school to college, have little or no contact with computers during their educational careers. This will change drastically in the coming years because computers are becoming integral parts of thousands of jobs. Few people will be able to find jobs that are not influenced, in one way or another, by computers.

Computer Literacy

This brings us to the first use of a computer: as a means of becoming computer literate. Although children tend to take to computers naturally, many adults are not at ease with them. They feel uncomfortable around them and do not look forward to the time when computers are an applicance in the home and office.

Buying and using a computer like the IBM PC is one very effective way of overcoming that initial feeling of discomfort. It is a good way to learn how the computer operates and what it can and can't do. Becoming computer literate is perhaps the most important educational benefit of owning a computer.

You may think computer literacy is silly because it implies understanding computers is like learning to read. Reading is an essential skill in this society, while computer literacy is not. However, the universal need to be able to read is a relatively modern concept. Two hundred years ago, well over ninety-nine percent of the world's population could not read. Yet these illiterate people were able to deal with their day-to-day demands. Arguing that everyone should be taught to read probably sounded silly in the 1700s. Today we believe the next generation should be taught to read because our society requires it. You cannot cope with life today as a responsible adult without that skill.

The shift from an *industrial* to an *information* society will continue and will bring us rapidly to the point where computer literacy is just as essential to modern living as reading.

Computer-Assisted Instruction

Computer-Assisted Instruction (CAI), Computer-Aided Learning (CAL), and Computer-Aided Instruction (CAI) are all terms that refer to the use of a computer in education. We will use the abbreviation CAI to refer to several types of computer-based teaching approaches that give some of the responsibility for teaching to the computer. There are three general types of CAI: drill and practice, tutorial, and simulations.

Drill and Practice

The simplest type of computer-assisted instruction is drill and practice. Drill and practice programs don't really teach you anything, they just help you practice something you've already learned. A common type of program helps you practice basic math skills. The computer generates a problem and asks the student to type in the answer. When you answer, the computer checks the answer for accuracy.

A more sophisticated type of drill and practice program keeps track of your errors. It explains errors and provides help. New problems are adjusted to your current needs. Some drill and practice programs set the difficulty level of problems on the basis of your performance during earlier sessions.

Tutorial Programs

A tutorial program does more than just give you practice on something you already know. It actually teaches. Educational programs that use the tutorial format are more difficult to write than drill and practice programs. You must teach the skill, evaluate learning, and provide practice. There are a few good tutorial programs for the IBM PC.

Simulations

When you drop a quarter into an arcade game and control an interstellar fighter with laser guns and force-field shields, you are participating in a computer simulation. Most of the arcade games are simulations.

Simulations are models of often complex events or conditions. You take a role in the simulation and help determine what happens next by the decisions you make. A computer simulation is an imaginary environment with its own rules. In an educational simulation, you take a role in the imaginary environment (for instance, as king of an ancient kingdom, as president of a large manufacturing company, or as operator of a small retail business). The decisions you make determine what happens next. In a popular simulation called *Hammurabi*, you are the ruler of an ancient city that has 100 citizens, 1000 acres of land for cultivation, and 3000 bushels of grain in storage. As ruler you must decide how much grain to give the people to eat, how much to save for seed, and how many acres to plant. Your decisions determine whether the kingdom starves, or grows and develops (and requires more grain the next year).

Simulations are widely used in business and industry. Nuclear and chemical plant workers are trained by computer simulations. It is much less expensive to have a trainee blow up a make-believe plant on the computer screen than to make a real mistake.

They are useful in teaching basic skills, concepts, and attitudes. Some are not only effective training tools, they are also fun. Many of the popular computer and arcade games are simulations designed for maximum enjoyment rather than learning aids. But as we noted in Chapter Two, there are some educational aspects of many of the popular video games.

Other Educational Applications

Computer literacy, drill and practice, tutorial programs, and simulations account for the majority of computer applications in education today. Another approach, Computer-Managed Instruction (CMI), uses the computer as a manager or overseer of learning. For example, students may be given a series of assignments that require them to read a text and work in the library. As each assignment is finished, the student sits at the computer and takes a test on the assignment. A "pass" means the student can go on to the next assignment. Otherwise, the computer provides suggestions for further study.

CMI requires quite a lot of work from the teacher to set up, but it does not require the teacher to actually write the programs. The teacher can use an *authoring language* to develop both CAI and CMI programs without learning to program the computer. Several authoring languages are available for the IBM PC. Miracle Computing, for example, sells *EasyLearn*, a program that helps you write educational software on your IBM PC. It is a versatile, inexpensive program that makes it easy to create drill and practice and tutorial software. The PILOT language, which is available for the IBM PC, is often used by teachers who want to develop their own CAI or CMI.

Another educational application has to do with the popular computer language, Logo. This language, developed at the Massachusetts Institute of Technology, is considered by many to be an ideal first language for children. Advocates say the language not only provides children with an enjoyable, even exciting, way to learn to program a computer. It also helps them develop better, more sophisticated ways of thinking and solving problems. Parents and teachers who would like to read a strong statement of support for Logo by its developer should read Seymour Papert's book, *Mindstorms*. A less enthusiastic, but still positive, view of the language is given in *Computers, Teaching, and Learning*, a book published by dilithium Press and written by Jerry Willis, LaMont Johnson, and Paul Dixon.

The computer is also a versatile *tool* in the classroom or at home. We use many tools in our efforts to learn: pens, pencils, tablets, rulers, and protractors. Specialized classes such as chemistry, biology, or typing also have their own set of tools: Bunsen burners, flasks, test tubes, scales, scalpels, and typewriters. The computer is likely to be an important educational tool in the future. English students will use its word processing power to write term papers, students in physics and chemistry will use it to calculate complicated formulas, and math students are likely to find it integrated into math courses. The computer's role as an educational tool is likely to grow in the future.

EDUCATIONAL SOFTWARE

Drill and Practice and Tutorial Programs

Currently, drill and practice programs are much easier to find than tutorial programs, but we will review both kinds of software in this chapter.

Cdex Training for the IBM Personal Computer

This is a three-disk tutorial from Cdex ($69.95) that helps you learn how to use the IBM PC. The program comes at-

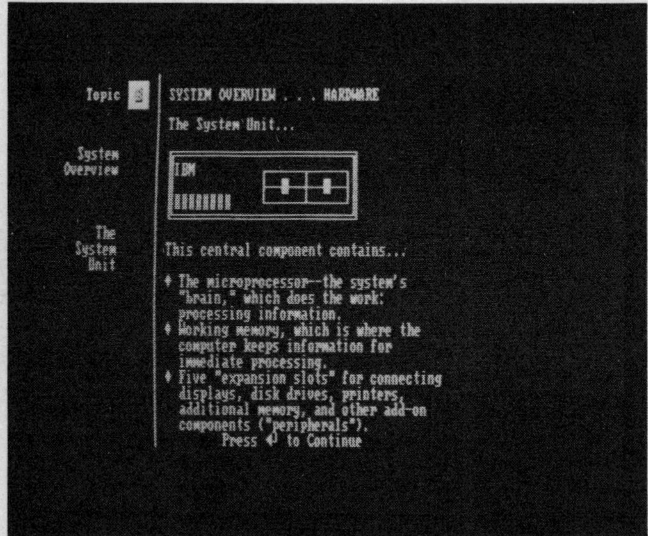

Figure 4.1   Cdex training for the IBM Personal Computer

tractively boxed, and the well-done manual comes in a three-ring binder. You will need 64K of memory, a monitor, and the IBM PC-DOS on diskette to use this program. The disk operating system is not necessary to run the training programs, but you will need it to carry out some exercises.

This training package was designed to be easy even if you know nothing about the IBM or any other computer. Directions in the manual begin by explaining how to turn the computer on and insert the disk. The program takes over from there. The first menu lets you choose from the following lessons: How to Use This Program, System Overview, First Contact, System Components, DOS, Using BASIC, System Details, Advanced DOS, Other Operating Systems and Languages, and Application Programs. After you choose the lesson you want, the program tells you what disk you need to insert.

The lessons themselves are well-done and basic. Text and diagrams are used, and the left side of the screen always displays the lesson and the specific subject being taught. After information is printed, you will be asked several multiple choice questions. If you get the answers right, the program proceeds. If you get one wrong, you are asked to try again, and you are led through a review of that material.

The same company also sells similar training programs for *VisiCalc*, *WordStar*, *SuperCalc*, and *EasyWriter II*.

Word Challenge

Word Challenge ($39.95) is a word game that gives you spelling practice. You need 64K and one disk drive to play this educational game. In this game, you compete with LEX (the computer). The task is to put together as many words as possible in three-minutes. The words must be at least three letters long.

In the standard game, the computer displays a four-by-four grid with a letter of the alphabet in each of the sixteen blocks. You press a key to start, and the computer displays the time remaining in the three-minute period. You type in as many words as you can find, while the computer does the same thing.

To prevent you from copying the computer's words, they appear only as question marks.

This is an interesting and enjoyable word game that could help you sharpen your spelling skills. The manual is excellent and the entire program is *menu-driven*: you are presented with multiple-choice screens when you start the game, to choose the difficulty level, and so on.

This is a flexible game. If you decide to play the standard game, you need only press one key. But you may decide to take advantage of the other options. You can choose one of twenty-six levels of difficulty, set your own grid, change the grid size to three-by-three or five-by-five, change the time interval for each round, choose to play the game in color, turn off the music and other sound effects, or take advantage of many other options.

Word Challenge is an entertaining game with an excellent manual. It has enough options so that it would be challenging

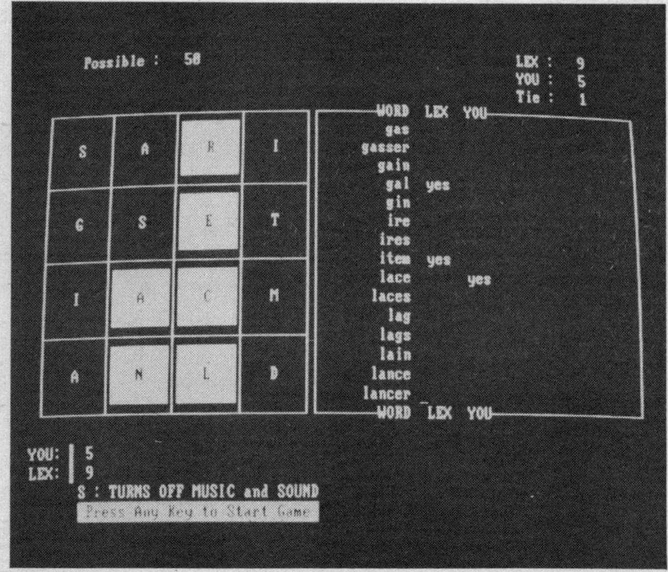

Figure 4.2   Word Challenge

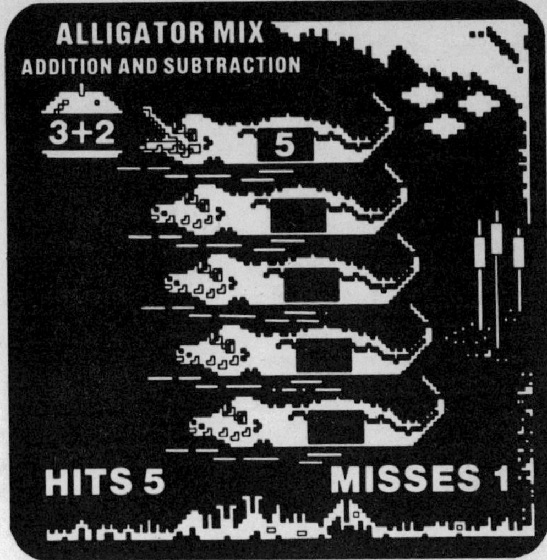

Figure 4.3   Alligator Mix

over a long period of time for both children and adults. We recommend this educational game from Proximity Devices.

Arcademic Skill Builders

This series of twelve disks combines some of the characteristics of arcade action games with drill and practice. They were developed by the DLM company, major producers of special education materials. Six of the games are language arts games, and six are math games.

These games sell for $34 each or $122.40 for the entire set. Each package includes a manual, a diskette with instruction sheet, duplication masters for use in schools, and a set of flashcards. As you can tell from the contents of each package, DLM is aiming these drill and practice packages at schools. Parents buy them, too, because they give children motivation to practice basic skills. These programs are a creative blend of education and gaming.

The math games include *Dragon Mix*, *Alligator Mix*, *Alien Addition*, *Demolition Division*, *Minus Mission*, and *Meteor Multiplication*. In *Meteor Multiplication*, you are given a multiplication problem. Your task is to blast the asteroid using the correct answer.

When the game begins, a high-quality color graphic of your star station appears in the center of the display. The star station is surrounded by eight colorful asteroids rapidly converging on the station. In the center of each asteroid is a multiplication problem like 6×6 or 4×2. The sound effect is a clock ticking.

With each tick, an asteroid blinks and moves one step closer to the space station. What you must do is type in the answer to the problem centered in an asteroid. The answer then appears in the center of the space station. You use the arrow keys to rotate the space station until its laser gun is pointed at the

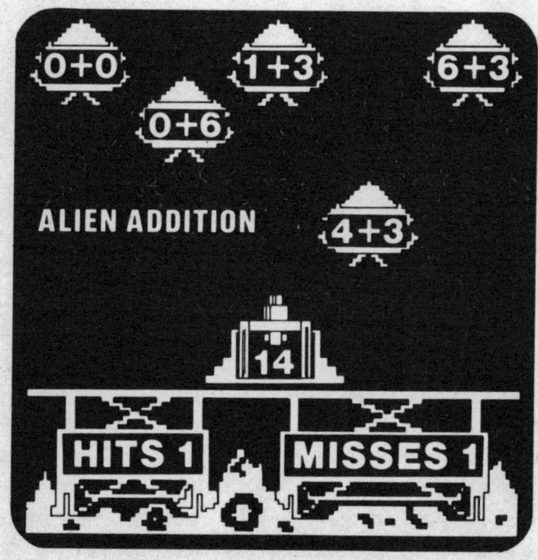

Figure 4.4   Alien Addition

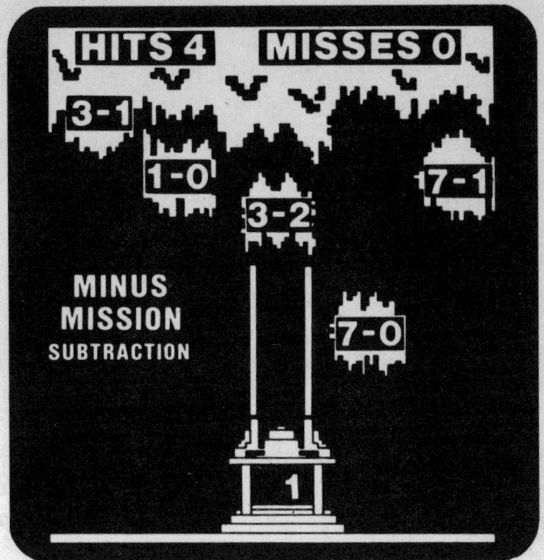

Figure 4.5   Minus Mission

approaching asteroid. You fire the laser by pressing the space bar. If you type in the correct answer, the asteroid disintegrates when you hit it, complete with satisfying sound effect. If the answer is wrong, the laser fires, but the asteroid continues to advance on the station. You must destroy all the asteroids before they reach the station. If any asteroid reaches the space station, you lose. Hits and misses are recorded at the bottom of the screen. High and low scores are displayed periodically.

In *Demolition Division*, five tanks displaying division facts between 0 and 9 move toward five artillery emplacements on the right side of the screen. As the tanks advance, they fire their guns at a wall protecting each gun emplacement. You enter a number beside one of your guns and hit the space bar. If the number is too large, your shot lands behind the tank. If the number is too short, the shot falls in front of it. If the number is the correct answer to the problems displayed by the tank, the tank is destroyed. You must work quickly, because when a wall is totally destroyed by a tank, the next shot wipes out the gun emplacement and you lose the game.

Dragon Mix gives practice in both multiplication and division facts. A large dragon on the right of the screen is defending a city with skyscrapers in the background. Three alien ships are approaching the dragon. Each ship has a different multiplication or division problem in it. An answer to one of the three problems appears in the center of the dragon. You must match the answer to the approaching ship, aim the dragon's tongue at it, and hit the space bar. If you choose the correct ship, it is destroyed. If you make the wrong choice, the ship just keeps coming. If a ship gets close enough, it begins to wipe out the city. Three hits on the city, and you lose.

The other programs are similar in content. You get the idea. Arcade-style action graphics and sound effects are used to keep the child motivated. Each diskette is programmed so that you

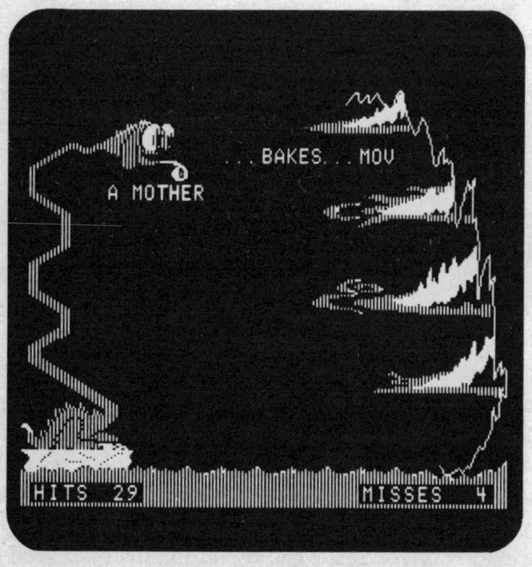

Figure 4.6   Verb Viper

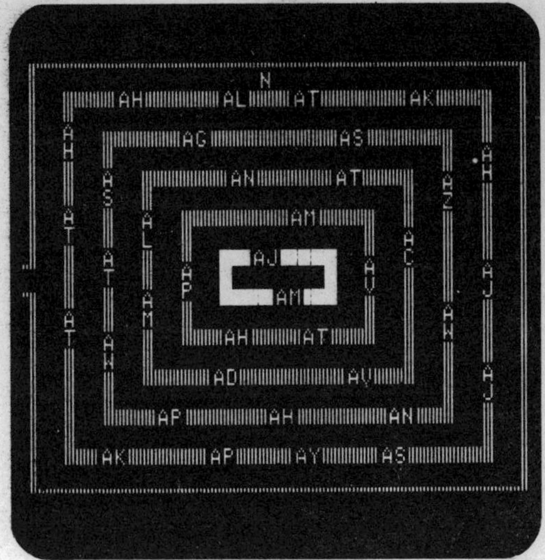

Figure 4.7   Word Man

can change the game in certain ways. Speed of action, difficulty
of problems, time for each game, and whether the keyboard
or game paddles are used can all be changed to suit your needs.

The language arts games are called *Verb Viper*, *Word Man*,
Word Invasion, *Spelling Wiz*, *Word Radar, and Word Master*.
These games focus on drill in verb tenses and subject-verb
agreement; word formation; identification of major parts of
speech; spelling; sight word recognition; and synonyms, an-
tonyms, and homonyms. These six games sell for $44 each or
all six for $158.40. If you purchase two to eleven games, you
receive a discount of forty percent off the per-unit price.

These games are unusually good in a couple of ways. First,
the graphics, the sound effects, and the action are truly first-
rate and enjoyable. Children and adults alike play these games
just for the fun of it. Other educational games have included
some action sequences, but too often they were poorly done,
graphics and sound effects (if any) were crude, and the games

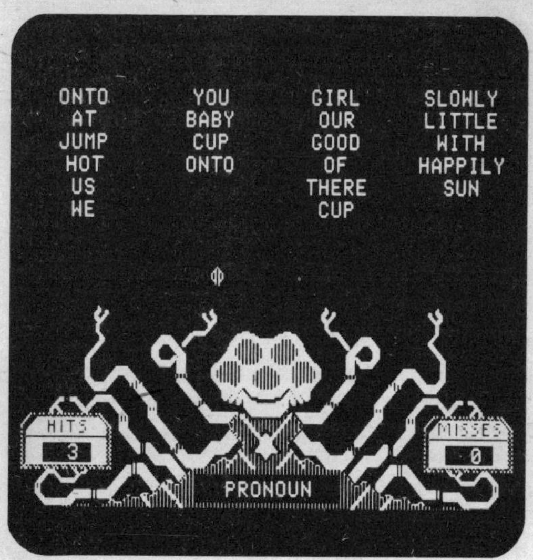

Figure 4.8   Word Invasion

were just plain boring. Not so with *Arcademics*. Second, in this series of games, the arithmetic drills are actually part of the game itself. The child must choose the correct answer to destroy the attacking meteors, for example. In many other games, action sequences are included only as a reward for completing the drill, and the educational content is not really part of that action. The games in the *Arcademics* series are not like that. The educational content plays an important role in the action sequences.

Some sound educational thinking went into this unique series of programs. Finding educational software incorporating both excellent programming and educational content is rare. DLM has both in this series.

College Board SAT Exam Preparation Series

This six-disk series ($299.95) has over forty programs designed to help you improve your score on the Scholastic Ap-

Figure 4.9   Spelling Wiz

titude Test (SAT). The SAT is the test used by many American colleges to help them determine who will be admitted as students. These programs generate questions similar to the questions used on the SAT and give you practice answering them. The computer is also programmed to give you quick feedback on how you're doing, along with explanations of any problems you don't understand.

Krell Software Corporation has produced an excellent set of programs. Menus are presented when lessons are started or finished, and instructions are easy to understand. Krell is so sure their program will result in improved performance on the SAT, that they issue a warranty. They promise to refund the full purchase price of the software if you use the programs but fail to increase your score by at least seventy points.

The six disks have drill and practice in skill areas tested by the SAT: math, vocabulary, written English, word relationships, reading comprehension, and sentence completion. There are two disks for math programs; two for English programs, one for vocabulary programs; and one for word relationships, reading comprehension, and sentence completion.

You may choose to use the *automatic learning strategy* for any of the programs. If you choose this option, the program analyzes your performance as you go and uses that information to change the way problems are selected. This helps you work at the level you need: not too hard and not too easy.

Another option, the *worksheet generator*, can be used if you have a printer. It produces a written copy of the problems and an answer sheet.

At the end of each session, you can choose to be shown a screen display or a printout telling you how you did on each type of skill covered by that lesson. This tells you how you are doing and what areas of study you need more work in.

This is an excellent way to practice for the SAT. If you are hoping to improve your score, we wouldn't be surprised if this program helps you do it. In addition, Krell is planning another interesting package for release in 1984. Called *Complete Class-*

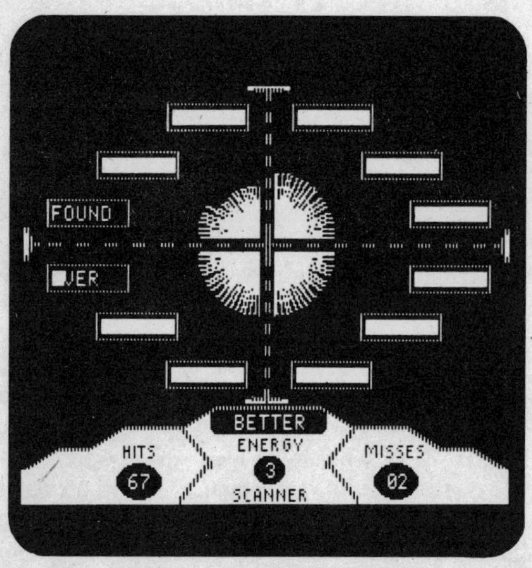

Figure 4.10   Word Radar

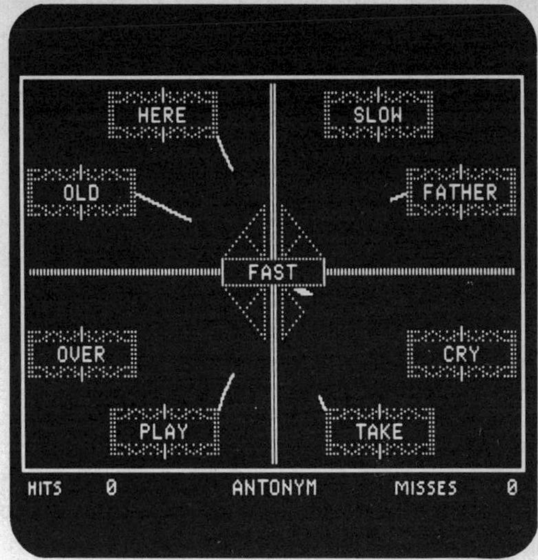

Figure 4.11   Word Master

room Tutorial Package, this series of programs will go beyond drill and practice to give detailed instruction in the specific skill areas needed to do well on the SAT. If Krell does as good a job on this tutorial package as it has done on its drill and practice package, this one will be another winner!

MasterType

The Universe is not always kind to those who type slowly. There is hope, however, for those who carefully read this manual. It is your guide to survival in interstellar combat.

So begins the *MasterType* manual. This is another program, this time a tutorial, that uses arcade action to help teach you a skill. There are eighteen lessons for $49.95. Each lesson teaches a different touch-typing skill. At the beginning of each lesson, the screen tells you what is being taught and gives you instructions on how good typists use that skill.

Most lessons feature you in the middle of a screen as a large blue command ship. You are being attacked by smaller enemy ships, usually from all four corners of the screen. A word or letter appears in each corner of the display, and you must type it. If you type it correctly, a bolt of energy flashes out from your ship and destroys an attacker. You can't relax, because the ships keep coming and new things to type keep appearing. If an attacker gets close enough to touch your ship, it is destroyed. The program keeps score, the graphics are excellent, and the sound effects are first-rate. It is published by Lightning Software.

M-SS-NG L-NKS and Other Programs

Sunburst Communications sells a number of educational programs for your IBM PC. *M-SS-NG L-NKS* is a series of programs aimed at teaching language skills to children and adults. They are really language puzzles that let students discover and put to work implicit language skills they may not even know they have. This program comes in seven versions:

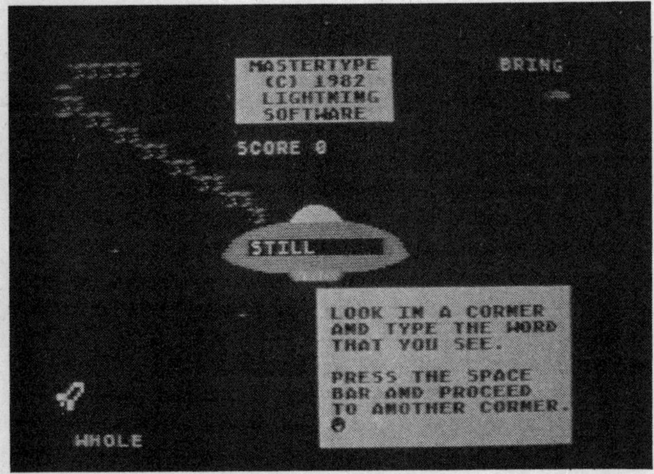

Figure 4.12   MasterType

Young People's Literature, *Literary MicroAnthology*, *MicroEncyclopedia* ($49.00 each); *English Editor*, *German Editor*, *Spanish Editor*, and *French Editor* ($59 each).

In all versions, children fill in the blanks in words and sentences using knowledge about the succession of letters in words, words in sentences, and the meaning of the whole.

This series of language programs was designed by a group of people who are experts in how children acquire language. The theory behind these programs is sound, the lessons are interesting and well-done, and we recommend them highly.

Other IBM programs available from Sunburst are *Survival Math* ($49) and *The Pond* ($49). *Survival Math* presents some interesting simulations, such as putting your child in charge of a hot dog stand. We'll talk about that program later. *The Pond* is a problem-solving program aimed at helping children and adults recognize and articulate patterns, generalize from raw data, and think logically. There are six levels of difficulty. You determine patterns of lily pads that will get a frog across a pond.

Sunburst has a large number of other educational programs

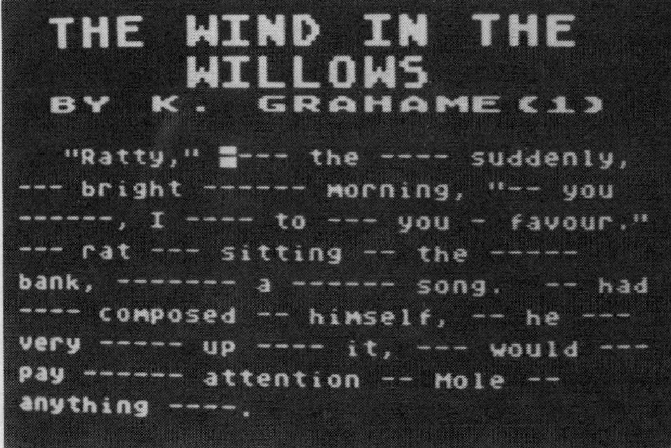

Figure 4.13   M-ss-ng L-nks

available in the $25–$60 price range. Write for a catalog if you're interested.

Shelby Lyman Chess Tutorial Series

Krell's new series of thirty-nine modules is not for casual chess players. This tutorial series sells for $39.95 *each* and is designed to help the serious student of chess improve. Space doesn't permit a complete listing of all thirty-nine modules, but some examples are *The Premature Attack: How to Refute It, Exploiting Pawn Weaknesses*, and *The Use of the King in Chess*.

These modules are computer implementations of the Socrates Chess Corporation's Shelby Lyman Chess Tutorial Series. Lyman is a chess expert and TV commentator well-known to chess buffs. Most individuals won't lay out the nearly $1500 for this entire series, but you may want to order just a few of

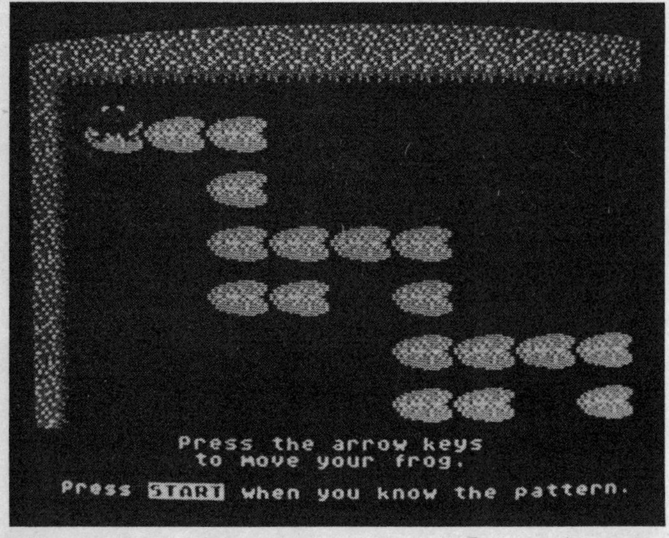

Figure 4.14   The Pond

these excellent tutorials to help you with specific parts of your game.

Creature Creator

Creature Creator is a computer game for preschool children. The skill this game teaches is pattern-matching, a fundamental skill for reading. Children are presented with a variety of heads, bodies, arms, and legs. They choose how they want to combine these parts to create their own personal monster. The monster can then be programmed to dance, jump, or hop around with another ghoulish friend. Colorful graphics and sound effects make this game popular with young children. *Creature Creator* lists for $39.95 from DesignWare.

The same company also markets *Spellicopter* for the IBM PC. This game drills children six years and older on visual memory and spelling skills. It also lists for $39.95.

An added benefit of buying software from this company is that you will receive a free quarterly newsletter for children who are interested in computers. *Kids' Computer News* is sent to anyone who returns the warranty card.

TellTime

TellTime is a free educational program by Lloyd Onyett printed in the March 1983 issue of *PC Magazine*. The program is designed to give children practice in telling time. You need a color monitor. When the program is run, it first displays a clock with hour and minute hands. Three possible times are spelled out below the clock, and the child attempts to choose the correct one. The correct time is rewarded with a pleasing tone and a happy face, while the incorrect choice brings an obnoxious tone and a sad face. This is an effective way for children to practice telling time.

This program is typical of the free programs printed in computer magazines. There's no such thing as a free lunch, of course, so there's a catch. To get this program, you'll have to type in the entire program (over 100 lines). This will take some time, and if you make errors, the program won't run. Nevertheless, there is satisfaction in getting a worthwhile program for the cost of a magazine.

Children as Programmers

Logo

Logo is a computer language written especially for children by Seymour Papert. Papert is an MIT computer scientist who studied child development for five years in Geneva, under the renowned child psychologist, Jean Piaget. Papert and his colleagues then developed Logo, based on Piaget's ideas about how children think and learn. In his book, *Mindstorms*, Papert suggests that if educational computing is to be of value, the child must program the computer, rather than the computer programming the child (as in drill and practice).

Logo makes it possible for children to actually program the computer to create complex graphics. Children are able to begin doing this after only a five- to ten-minute introduction to Logo commands! Papert believes that Logo can actually change the quality of children's thinking. While enjoying Logo, children learn mathematical and geometric concepts easily. We believe Logo holds great promise for educating children, and we recommend its use both at home and at school.

Although Logo will do other things besides create graphics, many people believe it is the graphics capabilities that are most important. Logo can be learned and used at many different levels of complexity.

Logo graphics revolve around a *turtle*, a triangular object that is guided around the screen with a series of simple commands. As the turtle moves, it leaves a line in its path. You can create complex designs by moving the turtle in this way. Additional commands can change the background color or the color of the lines drawn by the turtle.

Even if Papert is overly optimistic about changing the quality of children's thought, there are some other things to recommend Logo. Many children dislike school because they associate it with failure. Logo can give the child successful control of a complex instrument—the computer—at school. Logo can motivate the child to learn mathematical and geometric concepts in order to move the turtle efficiently. If errors are obvious right away, the computer is nonjudgmental. This is particularly good if the child is sensitive to adult criticism. Logo can also be used to encourage children to work as they attempt to solve Logo problems in groups.

A version of Logo is available for use on several computers with color displays. Up to now, we believe that the Texas Instruments' version has been best for most uses with young children, while an Apple version has been best for older children and adults. The situation may change soon, as several new versions of Logo are due to be introduced in late 1983 and early 1984. New versions of Logo will soon appear for the Aquarius color computer from Mattel Electronics, for the ATARI computers, for the Commodore 64 computer, and, thank goodness, for the IBM PC computer.

Gary Kildall, president of Digital Research and developer of DR Logo, says he expects Logo to replace BASIC as an all-purpose programming language. Review copies of this new version of Logo were not available when this book was written, but Kildall certainly makes it sound as if DR Logo is going to be a major version of Logo. The price will probably be around $150, and the package will include a cartoon-illustrated tutorial for children, as well an adult-oriented tutorial.

DR Logo will include more than 150 separate commands. You can write games, make charts, and do a variety of other tasks.

Facemaker

Facemaker is a unique program designed to introduce children to computer programming. The display presents a blank oval for a face and a list of facial features. Children can choose what features they want to add to the face, then what type of feature they prefer. For example, there are several types of hair, eyes, and mouths they can use.

Once they have constructed the face, they are given a very simple programming language consisting of one-letter commands. With these commands, the child can program the face to do things like wink, cry, smile, frown, and stick out its tongue. A program reading CFTTT would cause the face to cry, frown, and stick out its tongue three times.

We like this program. It seems to teach children to think logically, and they enjoy it greatly. *Facemaker* lists for $40 from Spinnaker Software.

Simulations

Simulations are computer-generated environments in which you can play a role. We have already discussed several simulation programs in the chapter on computer games (Chapter Two). We will discuss some more here.

Eliza

Eliza is a famous text-only program developed at the Massachusetts Institute of Technology in 1966 by Joseph Weizenbaum as part of MIT's artificial intelligence project. The program responds in a quasi-intelligent fashion to English language questions and statements you type on the keyboard.

The original use of this interesting program was to simulate a psychotherapist talking to a client (the computer is the therapist, you are the client). Weizenbaum reported the program functioned so realistically that the secretaries in his office eventually requested to be left alone with the computer so that they could work out their problems!

The version you can purchase for your IBM PC is fun and can be used to help learn about artificial intelligence. Here's an excerpt of a conversation with the program (Eliza's comments are printed in capital letters):

Men are all alike.
IN WHAT WAY?
They're always bugging us about something or other.
CAN YOU THINK OF A SPECIFIC EXAMPLE?
Well, my boyfriend made me come here.

YOUR BOYFRIEND MADE YOU COME HERE. THAT'S INTERESTING.
He says I'm depressed much of the time.
I AM SORRY TO HEAR YOU ARE DEPRESSED.
It's true. I am unhappy.
DO YOU THINK COMING HERE WILL HELP YOU NOT TO BE UNHAPPY?

Very impressive, right? This program is fun to play with. It isn't infallible, as the following excerpt illustrates:

HOW DO YOU DO?
PLEASE TELL ME YOUR PROBLEM.
I have a cold.
WHY DO YOU NEED TO TELL ME YOU HAVE A COLD?
You asked me.
WHY DO YOU THINK I ASKED YOU?
I can see the question on my CRT.
YOUR CRT—THAT'S INTERESTING.
No, it isn't.
WHY NOT?
Because I said so.
IS THAT THE REAL REASON?
Yes
YOU SEEM QUITE POSITIVE
I am
CAN YOU ELABORATE ON THAT?
No
ARE YOU SAYING NO JUST TO BE NEGATIVE?
Yes
YOU ARE SURE?
Yes
I SEE
What do you see?
WHY DO YOU ASK?
I'm curious
IS IT BECAUSE YOU ARE CURIOUS THAT YOU CAME TO ME?

I came to you because I'm bananas.
PERHAPS IN YOUR FANTASY WE CAME TO EACH
OTHER
Maybe you're the one who is bananas
YOU DON'T SEEM QUITE CERTAIN
Yes, now I am
I SEE

This may be as close as you ever get to turning the tables on *Eliza*! The program is available on disk for $25 from Artificial Intelligence Research Group.

Snooper Troops Case #1 and #2

These two Spinnaker programs each list for $44.95 and are intended to give children practice in taking notes and drawing maps, in classifying and organizing information.

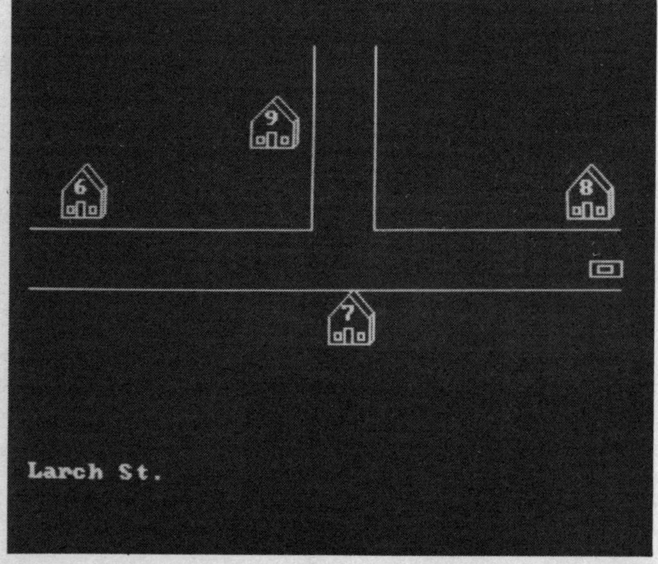

Figure 4.15   Snooper Troops Case #1

The two programs are detective simulations. Case #1 is called *The Granite Ghost*, and case #2 is called *The Disappearing Dolphin*.

As you've probably guessed, the object of these games is to solve the crimes. If you practice the skills listed above, you'll be able to do that, but it will take at least 12 hours for each crime. These games are for children ten years old and up. You can save the game any time you want to stop for awhile, then proceed later from where you left off.

We like these games. They have excellent color graphics and sound effects. They're a painless way to practice some important school-related skills.

Hot Dog Stand Survival Math

This program is an interesting text-only simulation from Sunburst Communications and lists for $50. It's based on the idea that people in many walks of life need some math ability to do their jobs well.

At the beginning of the program, you are told that your club is planning a hot dog stand at eight home football games. You have $200 to begin with, and your goal is to accumulate $2500. You must purchase hot dogs and buns, chips, soda, napkins, mustard, and relish and set the price for all items.

The computer determines the weather for the game and decides how many items were sold, calculates your profit and costs, and gives you your new bank balance. You continue until you reach your goal or until you go broke.

This interesting simulation could be used to plan for purchasing and price-setting for a real enterprise. It's fun, and you may learn some interesting facts about why you have to pay so much for that hot dog at the next football game you attend.

Sunburst Communications has some other interesting simulations. You might want to write and ask for a copy of their catalog.

Children and Word Processing

Another educational use of computers is word processing (see Chapter Seven). Children, or anyone else who wishes to improve their writing skills, can profit from word processing. It makes the mechanics of revision easy and encourages you to experiment. Then, too, spelling and grammar checkers find errors easily, and they can be corrected without submitting the paper to the critical eye and red pencil of a teacher.

To benefit the most from word processing, you need to be at least a fairly good typist, so we recommend a good typing tutor along with a word processing package.

ADDITIONAL SOURCES
OF INFORMATION

Some magazines you may be interested in include *Computers in the Schools*, *The Computing Teacher*, and *Educational Computer Magazine*.

Other magazines especially helpful to IBM PC owners are *PC World*, *PC Magazine*, and *Softalk*.

CHAPTER FIVE

Home Finance, Record Keeping, and Health Care

PUT YOUR IBM PC TO WORK AT HOME

Most people don't buy a computer specifically for the uses described in this chapter but for some other reason like word processing, telecommunications, and playing games. You will probably get a computer for other purposes, and then begin looking for more ways to use it. There is a wide variety of software in this area, though. We will discuss some of it in this chapter. By watching the ads and reviews in computer magazines, you can become aware of new software as it becomes available.

Interface Age magazine led the way in describing home applications of the microcomputer. Their December 1977 issue has two articles by Francis Ascolillo on a *Household Finance System*. Written in BASIC, the program can give your family an overview of spending and earning patterns. When you write your family checks each month, you simultaneously give the computer the data needed to do an analysis. Monthly and yearly printouts show your spending patterns and predicted trends. The same issue has a personal accounts payable program written in BASIC by Kevin Redden. With it you can keep track of bills received, payments made, and information like time between receipt and payment, minimum payment due, total amount owed on each account, and interest paid on each account. These BASIC programs can be adapted for your IBM PC (see Chapter Nine on Programming), or you may purchase similar programs written especially for the IBM PC.

Many of the popular computer magazines regularly publish programs for the IBM PC in this category. A well-stocked bookstore will carry at least two or three magazines with listings of software for the IBM PC.

The IBM PC as a Home Financial Manager

A growing number of programs are available that help home computer owners make personal financial decisions: budget control, financial planning, checkbook balancing, analysis of loan options, and filing income tax forms.

Tax Preparer

Tax Preparer is an excellent program designed to prepare, edit, and print the income tax forms and schedules most widely used by individuals. These forms include Form 1040, Schedules A through G, the Credit for the Elderly Form, the Social Security Self-Employment Tax Form, the Deduction for Married Couples When Both Work Form, and Forms 2106, 2119, 2210, 2441, 3468, 4562, 4625, 4797, 5695, and 6251.

All arithmetic computations are performed automatically, including the computation of all taxes from tables or tax rate schedules. You only need to enter new information, and all changes caused by new entries are made automatically on all affected forms.

This is a sophisticated program with many features. There is even a form letter giving brief filing instructions to clients you prepare returns for. Low-cost updates are available for each new year.

The cost of this tax-deductible program is $250. If you prepare your own taxes, we think you'll find this program from Howard Software Services helpful. You'll need at least 64K of memory and one disk drive to run *Tax Preparer*.

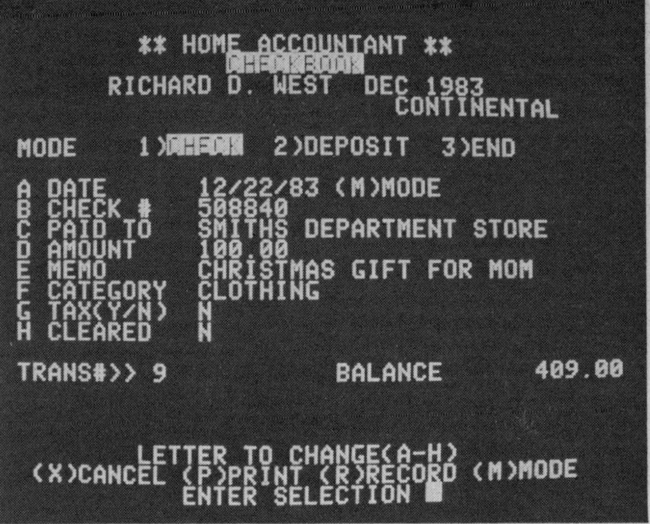

Figure 5.1   The Home Accountant

The Home Accountant

The Home Accountant, available for $150 from Continental Software, will help you get a clear and accurate picture of your financial condition at any time. You will see how much money is coming in and exactly where it is being spent. You can mark financial transactions so they can be used for tax purposes, and you can even print checks.

The budget module is the heart of this package and is extremely flexible. You can set up a complex budget if you choose, or you may wish to use the program only to keep track of your checking account. If you opt for a more complex budget, you can have as many as 100 budget categories within five broad budgeting areas: assets, credit cards, liabilities, income, and expenses. *The Home Accountant* gives you totals on all areas and categories. At the end of the year, you generate a report that summarizes your income, your expenditures, and your net worth.

You can break the five general categories down into more specific categories if you choose. For example, you may want to make utilities a separate category, with gas, electricity and water expenses a subcategory. The more detailed you make your records, the better you will be able to trace your financial affairs.

Once you have decided what information you want to enter, you use the *transactions module* to enter the data and to assign the budget categories. You also use this module to search or edit your data. The transaction module also helps you set up automatic transactions—things like rent payments that you want automatically deducted from your account each month.

You can use the *graphing module* to prepare graphs of your financial data. You can create bar graphs, line graphs, and trend analysis. The bar graph will display a comparison between budgeted amounts and actual amounts for any of the categories you have entered. Graphs must include a minimum of two months of financial activities.

You use the *printed reports module* to get various kinds of printed statements of your financial affairs. You can get reports such as budgeted amounts versus actual amounts, a personal balance sheet, and a net worth statement.

The *print checks/activity report module* can be used to print out a report of all transactions, or it can be used to print checks. You must use special checks.

You use the *start new year module* at the end of the year to prepare a new data disk and transfer all relevant information from the previous year.

The *extend module* is used if you have more than 1000 transactions in a year. This module prepares a new disk for additional transactions.

The *hardware/start new system module* holds information about your particular printer and has a program for start-up.

Personal Needs Analysis and Comparative Policy Analysis

These two programs from Insurance Micro Software help you decide what type of insurance you should carry and how much. They also help you analyze the comparative merits of different policies.

REAP

REAP stands for *Real Estate Activities Program*. If you own or are thinking about buying income property, this program can help you figure out how different options, such as methods of financing and methods of sale, affect your property.

REAP figures out how much return on equity you can expect and adjusts this figure by taking tax consequences into consideration. The program will also estimate your income tax payments and perform other tax-related estimates. The program lists for $39.95 from BV Engineering.

Real Estate Analyzer

A more sophisticated program called *Real Estate Analyzer* is available from Howard Software Services for $250. This program helps you make buy, hold, and sell decisions; it provides detailed analyses on real estate decision data, and it gives printouts in many different formats. The manual for this program is well-organized and informative. If you make substantial investments in real estate, this program would be very useful.

Chequemate Plus

This program helps you keep track of every type of home expenditure. You can make separate entries for transactions involving checks, credit cards, and automated teller transactions. It keeps track of accounts payable, gives help with budgeting, generates graphs of your financial transactions, and can produce income statements. It costs $150. You will need 48K, one disk drive, and a printer to run this program from Masterworks Software.

The Record-Keeping IBM PC

You can keep records of many things at home using your microcomputer. You can buy software for everything from keeping track of recipes to storing bartending instructions.

Data-Writer

Data-Writer is a personal record-keeping system available for $225. You can use this computer-based filing system by itself or with a word processor. You can set up a database, as well as a form letter and mailing list system. The program gives you a fast, easy way to create, maintain, and use your own customized files. Because it's a general record-keeper, you can tailor it to fit your own needs. It can be used for recipes, tax records, shopping lists, Christmas card lists, and for many other purposes.

You can use it to organize and set up customized files or update and rearrange existing files. You can print or display selected lists of file data or create a subset of a larger list. For example, if you have created a file of your exotic pressed flower collection, you can call up the files for all red orchids gathered on South Pacific atolls between one and two a.m. during a full lunar eclipse!

The program also has the ability to alphabetize entries or sort numbers (like zip codes) into ascending or descending order (great for bulk mailings), and there's even a subprogram for printing mailing labels.

Micro Cookbook

This cookbook program requires 64K and one disk drive and lists for $40. *Micro Cookbook* is actually far more than a cookbook. Oh, sure, it includes more than 200 international recipes, and there are already two add-on disks available with specialized recipes (*Appetizers* and *Soups and Salads*, $12 each). But the program itself is what makes *Micro Cookbook* special.

In the first place, the program is easy to use. For instance, it's completely menu-driven (what else would a cookbook program be?). Not only is it easy to use, but you can do so much with it! You can add all your own favorite recipes. You can tell the cookbook how many are coming for dinner, and it will automatically adjust the ingredient amounts. You can tell the program what ingredients you have in the house, and the program will tell you recipes you can prepare. You can display nutrition and calorie guides and a glossary of cooking terms. You can even print a shopping list by telling the program what meals you have in mind for the week!

Family Roots

Family Roots is a set of programs written to help you in your search for family historical information. You use a standard format to enter information about each family member. This information can be quickly and easily updated as it changes or as you discover new facts. The program lets you view and print this information in a variety of helpful ways.

The program asks you things like birth, death, marriage, occupation, offspring, and notes for each person. You may elect to print automatically-generated genealogy charts for both ancestors and descendants. There is even an electronic card file system for storing notes that don't fit into the basic categories.

This is a well-thought-out package that should be a real aid if you're into genealogy. The programs are menu-driven, and the manual is clear and well-organized. The touches of humor in the manual are welcome and do not detract from the information.

There are many supplementary packages available from the publisher of *Family Roots*, and there's a user's group. For example, *Lineages* sells for $102.50 and is intended to get you started in genealogy research. If you find you are going to stick with it, you can upgrade to *Family Roots*. The list price for *Family Roots* is $188.

Using Your Computer for Home Health Care

Home health care is a promising new area for home computer use. Although there isn't a great deal of software available in this area, we expect the future to bring increased interest and, consequently, much more software related to home health care.

NODVILL Diet Program

This handy diet program sells for $69.95 (NODVILL Software) and is intended to help you be sure that you are eating healthfully. It will also help you plan nutritious meals.

You must determine your approximate energy expenditure and enter it in the program. The manual lists a variety of activities under the low, medium, and high energy levels. For example, lying down or sleeping is a low energy activity that burns off only about eighty calories per hour. Running is a high energy activity that burns off about 900 calories per hour. (There are no statistics listed for compulsive computing.) The program also prompts you for less interesting but more objective data such as name, age, weight, and height. The program then shows you your nutritional requirements in units of vitamins and minerals.

A subprogram shows you how to enter the types of food you like and displays the nutritional content of the food, including how many calories it has. Over 700 foods are included, and you can add the data for sauteed hummingbird wings or other personal favorites not in the program. Another subprogram helps you plan meals for seven days, and another uses the menus you have generated to print out a shopping list.

Diet

Diet is a much less sophisticated and less expensive program to help you plan you and your family's diet. The program will ask you for personal data and use it to figure out what your daily caloric needs are. The program from Metamorphics, Inc. sells for $25. A similar program called Eatsmart is available from Executive Software Programming.

More Than 32 BASIC Programs for the IBM Personal Computer

An especially good software bargain is available for $34.95. *32 Basic Programs* (dilithium Press) comes with a full-length book by Tom Rugg and Phil Feldman, and a disk with thirty-six programs. The package includes educational graphics and math programs, as well as games and programs for home use.

Some of the home programs include *Biorhythm, Checkbook, Loan,* and *Mileage. Decide* is designed to help you make decisions involving the selection of one alternative from several choices. It works by prying relevant information from you and then organizing it in a meaningful, quantitative manner. Your best choice will be indicated and the possibilities given a relative rating.

You can use *Decide* for a wide variety of decisions. It can help with things like choosing the best stereo system, saying yes or no to a job or business offer, or selecting the best course of action for the future. The program personalizes the decision-making process.

The unique thing about this package is the documentation. Since all thirty-six programs, written in BASIC, are listed in their entirety, it is extremely easy to revise them if you wish. If not, the book does a great job of teaching you to use them as-is.

CHAPTER SIX

Tapping into the World: Telecommunications

You are probably aware of the video game potential of personal computers. You know that those desktop marvels playing *PAC-MAN*, *Frogger*, and *Fast Eddie* can do an honest day's work as word processors, accounting machines, and educational tools. The subject of this chapter is not so well known. Telecomputing involves connecting your home computer to other computers over standard phone lines. Your computer becomes a link to hundreds, perhaps thousands of other computers that have been programmed for various services. You can sit back in your easy chair, get a comfortable grip on your keyboard, and do everything from pay bills to read weather reports for Colorado ski resorts.

Telecomputing is one of the fastest growing areas of personal computer use. Many IBM PC owners regularly use their computer to talk to other computers. To begin telecomputing, you must connect your computer to a special device called a *modem*. The modem is connected to your phone line. You dial another computer's number, and when it answers, you talk to the computer by typing on the IBM PC keyboard. The computer on the other end of the phone line responds to your requests by sending information that is displayed on the television or monitor screen.

Because you may not be familiar with telecommunications, we will give you a somewhat extended introduction to the topic.

We'll explain the concept of telecommunications, give some examples of how it can be used, and tell you about the equipment and software you need to get started.

Telecommunications is complicated. There are many aspects of this phenomenon and many ways you can take advantage of the services. Trying to explain it is a little like trying to explain reading and talking. These are really *tools* that, if you have them, let you do many different things—from reading the morning paper to decoding the assembly instructions that come with Christmas toys. Telecommunications also gives you many ways to acquire and use information. Over the last century, the development of wireless communication technology such as radio, television, and satellite transmission systems changed the way we get much of our information. It also changed the type of information we get. Today, if you have cable television, you can tune to an all-news channel and get instant information on current news stories. Cable channels now or soon available will give you specific types of information in areas such as health and nutrition and business news.

Cable-based information systems all share one problem, however. You are a passive viewer with no direct control over the material you view. Yes, you can tune to the health and nutrition news channel, but it may or may not do a piece on the particular topic you want to hear about. Telecommunications will help you take a much more active role in the selection of information.

MAJOR TELECOMMUNICATIONS APPLICATIONS FOR HOME COMPUTERS

Telecommunications is actually a whole family of services you can get in your home or business if you have the proper equipment. There are a number of types of service; we will describe the major ones here.

What are Information Utilities?

When you go to your kitchen sink to get a glass of water, you simply turn on the tap, and out flows the water. A similar thing happens when you turn on the electric lights in your home or when you tune into your favorite cable television station. Water, electricity, and cable television services are called *utilities*. A utility service becomes available to you when you have the proper receiving equipment: the kitchen sink, the electric light, or the television set. Telecommunications can be thought of as a large family of information utilities that can be brought into your home or office through your personal computer. We will use the term *information utilities* in a very broad sense to include any source of information that can be accessed by a computer through telecommunications. Sometimes the term information utilities just describes very large systems that offer a wide variety of services. We like to think of an information utility as any kind of information service, large or small, local or national.

Starting with this definition of an information utility, we can say that many are now offered and many more will become available soon. To receive such a service, you will need the right equipment, and you will need to make the appropriate connections. In most cases, you will need to pay a utility fee, although some of these services are free. More detail will be given on how all this works later, for now let's look at some of the services available for your computer.

Local Area Networks
and Computer Bulletin Boards

There are hundreds of local computer *networks* now operating in this country. Most use regular phone lines for communications. They're run by universities and colleges, computer clubs, amateur radio clubs, and special interest groups. Members of the sponsoring organization (or, in some cases, anyone who knows the phone number) interact with the network's computer. Some systems limit use to reading the local electronic bulletin board; others let you use a large computer system's power from your own home.

A typical local area network will be sponsored by a computer club. The club pays for a phone line connected to the club's computer. When you call, the computer answers the phone electronically and asks what information you would like to have transmitted to your computer. There may be options such as reading the latest issue of the club's newsletter, browsing through want ads for used equipment, or looking at material written by other IBM PC owners about new products or problems. The type of network and the services offered vary greatly from one locale to the other. Local computer stores and computer clubs are usually aware of the networks operating in the area and what they offer. Many local networks are the electronic equivalent of the bulletin board down at the laundromat or at the factory, with notices of events, want ads, offers of free puppies or kittens, and descriptions of new computer equipment.

National Networks and Bulletin Boards

Besides local computer bulletin boards, several national systems (some with toll-free numbers) are available for the cost of the phone call. National bulletin boards are generally intended for a special audience, and some charge a fee. For example, HEX (Handicapped Education Exchange), reached by dialing (301) 593-7033, is used by individuals and organizations to exchange information on how technology can be used to help the handicapped. There are also national networks for owners of a particular brand of computer. Some of the IBM PC networks are described in a later section of this chapter.

Recreational Games

Both CompuServe and The Source, telecomputing department stores discussed later in this chapter, have provisions for playing games. Dial their numbers, type in your personal identification code, then play any of over 100 different games. Most games are the adventure or strategy type with little or no graphics, because it is difficult to transmit graphics quickly over phone lines and virtually impossible, without specialized software, to transmit usable graphics to all the different models of personal computers on the market today.

Downloading Programs

Several networks sell programs by *downloading* them to your computer and billing the cost to a credit card. Some services even let you try the program first; if you like it, the program is yours for a small fee. Before you can download programs, you must buy a special program that lets you store the programs you buy on a cassette or disk. Downloading services for owners of IBM PC computers are not common today, but the number is growing.

Databases

A database is simply a batch of information stored in the memory of a computer. If you need to know the current price of IBM stock or the time of the next plane to Lubbock, this information—and much more—is available from databases provided by information utilities. Both The Source and CompuServe have such information stored in extensive databases. A service called DIALOG has hundreds of specialized databases. A doctor can check on a recommended treatment for a new disease, a farmer can get predictions on the wheat crop in South America, and a consumer can check discount prices on a dishwasher or color television.

Some writers predict that these large computerized information utilities, with their huge databases, will replace traditional sources of news and information such as newspapers and television newscasts. We doubt that. Newspapers are sources of professionally packaged and conveniently presented general information. We think information utilities are likely to be added to our existing sources of information rather than replacing them.

The reason for our view is that information utilities are not easy to access; it takes some effort to get information from them. In addition, they are not very convenient sources of general information. The morning paper or the nightly news gives us that. What information utilities do best is give us access to specific information. Suppose you are a member of a local group formed to fight for modifications in local laws governing waste disposal near the subdivision where you live. One task the group must accomplish is writing a booklet on the problem to be distributed to citizens and local officials. You want the booklet to be technically accurate, and you want to be able to include information on what has happened in other areas that faced a similar problem.

You could gather the background and support information you need by going to the library and searching through the relevant indexes for articles and books on the topic. However, a hand search would probably take a day or two of hard work at the library. Because it takes so long to do the search, it is not likely to be as comprehensive as it should. An alternative is a computerized search through a database available from an information utility called DIALOG (described later). A DIALOG search will give you a list of articles (with abstracts or summaries of the articles) and books on the topics of interest. A DIALOG search takes less than an hour and is more comprehensive. Even a DIALOG search is unlikely to point you to recent news stories on the topic. Those stories can be accessed through general information utilities like The Source or CompuServe.

Hundreds of these databases available through information

utilities today are of interest to professionals in virtually every field. You can use your IBM PC to find information on new metallurgical patents, federal court cases, space games, college scholarships, and much more.

Banking and Shopping

Several banks, led by the United American Bank of Knoxville, have systems that help customers transfer funds and pay bills by computer. Dial the bank's number, type in your account number, then type in the instructions on how much to pay whom. Chemical Bank of New York even has provisions for making purchases like airline tickets. The tickets are mailed to you and debited to your account. Some experts foresee *banking by computer* as a commonplace activity in the future. At present it is limited to a few areas where it is being test marketed and to people who use information utilities such as CompuServe.

Shopping by computer has caught the public's eye. There are several shopping services that help you order items that are charged to your credit card and mailed to your home or office. Both The Source and CompuServe have shopping services that will be discussed later. In addition, many services have various types of consumer information, such as movie and book reviews, and restaurant reviews.

Electronic Mail and Teleconferencing

Electronic mail means different things to different people. A large corporation may have computers that store messages written in the Dallas office to staff in the Chicago office. Late at night the Dallas computer automatically calls up the Chicago computer and transmits the messages. When the recipient of a message arrives at work the next day, a flashing light on the computer console indicates a message is waiting in the computer's memory. This is electronic mail.

Public access electronic mail involves typing a message to a friend on your keyboard. That message is sent to a company that handles electronic mail. The company transmits the message to the city where your friend lives. The message may then be printed out and delivered by the Post Office the next day. In the future your friend may have a home computer that is always connected to the phone line. Messages may be transmitted directly to your home and printed out on a printer attached to the computer.

Today a form of electronic mail is possible through the information utilities. Each person with an account has a user number that is an electronic address. If you need to send a report to a friend or colleague who lives across the country, you can transmit the report from your computer to The Source. When your friend next uses The Source, a message is waiting. The report is then transmitted from The Source to your friend, who can transfer it from the computer's memory to a disk or cassette.

MAJOR INFORMATION UTILITIES

Currently there are two established national general-purpose information utilities: The Source and CompuServe. Both can be used by anyone with a personal computer, a credit card (so they can bill you), and a telephone. Calls to the two major networks are local calls in many major cities because you are connected to them through special electronic communication networks—usually Telenet or Tymnet.

The Source

The Source is a service of Source Telecomputing Corporation. If you want to sign up, you can do so through the mail or at many computer stores. As with cable television, there is an initial hookup fee ($100). After that, The Source charges $7.75 per hour of use during non-business hours, less for late night use, $5.75, and during office hours, $20.75. There is a minimum monthly charge of $10 whether you use the system or not. The phone call to The Source is a local one in over 300 cities.

Few people will want every service offered by The Source, now a subsidiary of Reader's Digest, but it's nice to know they're there. Here are some of the most interesting services:

• *Electronic Mail.* Besides the method of electronic mail described earlier, it is possible to dial a toll-free number and dictate a letter over the phone. Your letter is put in the electronic mail file and will be available to the recipient the next time that person signs on. Special interest groups can also use the electronic mail feature by placing information in a sort of electronic bulletin board that can be read by subscribers with similar interests. There is also an electronic equivalent of junk mail. You type in a letter or report and tell the system to send it to as many Source subscribers as you wish.

• *Electronic Travel Service.* You can make your own airline and hotel reservations, get restaurant rating guides, and see international airline schedules. You have access to worldwide airline flight information updated every two weeks. If you are going to visit either New York or Washington, D.C., you can get listings of services ranging all the way from fur rental to babysitting before you leave home. One part of this service, called the Travel Club, can be used just like a travel agency. You can wrap up all your travel plans by asking the Travel Club to order tickets and make reservations.

• *Education.* The Source has a few drill and practice programs on a variety of topics suitable for both children and adults. Programs to teach spelling, math, foreign language, and science are available. There is a directory of financial support possibilities for college students, and a job service that lets you type in your resume so prospective employers can review it. There is also a jobs-available listing.

• *Consumer Aids.* You can get some informative articles on how to reduce energy costs and save gasoline and some assistance in choosing the right wines or the right vitamins. One part of this service called Comp-U-Store amounts to an electronic supermarket. You can review items and prices on the computer screen and place your order by typing on the computer keyboard. Then there is TradeNet, a barter service. With TradeNet, you can barter trips, professional advice on a range of subjects, and items of almost any description. The service also has restaurant guides and reviews for most large cities, and a movie review section.

• *Sports News*. You can get up-to-the-minute news on sports, team standings, sports trivia, and sports records, as well as round-ups of scores on a national, international, and statewide level.

• *Financial Services*. Business and financial forecasts from professional economists and security analysts are up-dated weekly.

• *Portfolio Management*. You have access to a system to create and maintain your personal investment portfolio. By simply entering a file name, you will see an up-to-date report on each stock in your portfolio.

• *Legi-Slate*. You can track bills referred out of Congressional committees and identify members of Congress by state, party, committee, and subcommittee. This service is up-dated weekly.

• *Commodity News Service, Inc*. This service helps you track price movements in commodities futures markets and gives you market commentary and commodity news.

• *Computing Services*. You can write and run programs in a variety of languages, including BASIC, COBOL, Pascal, and FORTRAN, among others. The Source also makes available a few canned programs. Many are free; some involve a small extra charge. The programs include games, business software, and software for special applications, such as statistical analysis of large amounts of data. You cannot buy these programs and run them without being connected to the service. In essence, you *rent* them by connecting to The Source by phone and typing in the name of the program you want to use.

• *Databases*. There are many other databases available on The Source. One of the more popular databases is the United Press International (UPI) wire service. You can tell The Source to put the UPI output on the screen, then watch the news scroll by a line at a time. However, that is an inefficient way of finding the news you're interested in. From your computer you can tell the UPI database exactly what stories you want to read. If you want information on what is happening in the latest crisis in any country, you can do so by typing in the name of the country. All of the recent stories filed with UPI about that country will be displayed. It is easy to get in-depth reports on any subject you are interested in. Best of all, you can have up-to-date information any time you want it. The UPI database is only one of many databases available on The Source. It takes some effort to learn how to use them effectively, but the effort is well worth it.

Many of the databases available on the system are oriented toward a particular topic. A person interested in the stock market, for example, can get detailed news and background information relevant to the companies he or she is interested in. There are databases on commodities, stocks, bonds, precious metals, and more. There is an electronic version of the magazine *U.S. News and World Report*, as well as abstracts of articles from magazines like *Forbes* and *Harvard Business Review*.

CompuServe

The major competitor to The Source is CompuServe Information Service, now a subsidiary of H & R Block. There are many similarities between the two major information utilities, and some differences. CompuServe has an initiation fee of around $30 and charges $5 per hour during non-business hours. The hourly rate is much higher during normal working hours. The connect call is a local one in over 300 cities.

CompuServe offers services similar to those of The Source. Instead of UPI, CompuServe uses the Associated Press newswire, and it has electronic editions of papers such as the *St. Louis Post-Dispatch*. There are also electronic editions of popular magazines such as *Computers and Electronics*, *Better Homes and Gardens*, and *Popular Science*. CompuServe also has a special interest group for IBM computer owners. It is one way to get up-to-date information on the IBM PC and other IBM computers.

CompuServe also offers information on topics as diverse as home repair, personal health, and recipes. Like The Source, it has book and movie reviews, as well as a sports information service. There is even a file of computer art that can be copied on your printer.

Like The Source, CompuServe has many financial databases you can use to investigate and track the performance of stocks and commodities. There is also a way of doing electronic banking on CompuServe through a bank in Boston or Knoxville. There is an electronic version of the *World Book Encyclopedia* on line, a program that helps you select a college, and a service called *Refundle Bundle* for coupon clippers.

CompuServe sign-up kits are available from some computer stores and many Radio Shack stores, or you can contact the main office directly. If a store in your area has the sign-up kits, all you have to do is fill out the paperwork, and you will get your account numbers. With the right equipment, you can then go home and begin using CompuServe. The base fee is $20, but you buy at least $10 worth of manuals to help learn how to use CompuServe. A CompuServe Starter Kit including manuals and several hours of time is $40.

Both CompuServe and The Source add new services regularly and both offer value for the money you pay.

OTHER INFORMATION UTILITIES

Besides the general-purpose information supermarkets, there are many specialized services. What they lack in breadth is more than offset by their depth.

Bulletin Boards for the IBM PC

You can log onto several bulletin boards for IBM PC owners, including one in Virginia at (703) 560-0979, one in Maryland at (301) 949-8848, and one in California at (213) 296-5927. When you use these bulletin board services, you can download programs from them. Don't expect to find a $200 piece of software that you can download free, however. Most of the programs you get from these services are hobby programs written by other IBM PC owners. There will be some good ones and some bad ones. The only cost to you is the long-distance telephone charge while the program is downloading.

One problem with small specialized bulletin boards is that they are often short-lived. Someone may start a good bulletin board, run it for several months, and then, for one reason or another, drop it. The best way to keep up on bulletin boards is to watch for listings in the computer magazines.

Knowledge Index

This is a special microcomputer version of DIALOG Information Service. DIALOG has a huge computer complex using billions of references on every imaginable subject. Due to the high cost of the DIALOG service, it is used primarily by professionals at libraries and universities. You use it to find out all about a certain subject. You don't have to go to the library and search through references, books, and magazines. The computer does all the searching and gathers the information for you. Knowledge Index costs $35 for the initial sign-up. With this initial fee, you get two hours of search time. After that, it costs $24 an hour to use the system.

Dow Jones News/Retrieval Service

You can join this service for an initial fee of $50. There is no monthly fee, but you are charged for the time you use the system. This charge varies, depending on how much service you use. This information utility has many different services, most of them related to financial and investment matters.

Money DOS

You can access this free service just by dialing the telephone number, once you are set up for telecommunications with the IBM PC computer. Money DOS is a bulletin board on financial investments. J. M. Keynes, a senior vice president of investments for a member firm of the New York Stock Exchange, offers this bulletin board. You can contact the bulletin board by dialing (305) 655-2340 during the week and on weekends by dialing (305) 655-3389. With your IBM PC computer set up for telecommunications, you can receive Mr. Keynes's latest advice, and if you have a printer, you can have it printed out for later reference.

The Encyclopaedia Britannica

You can search through the full text of the *Britannica 3* encyclopedia and the ten-volume *Micropedia*. The *Micropedia* is a capsule form of the encyclopedia. Other special editions such as *Book of the Year* are also included.

GETTING ON LINE

Does one or more of the possibilities in telecommunications arouse your interest? Would you like to use your IBM PC to connect yourself to a bulletin board or information utility?

Connecting the IBM PC to the Telephone

Once you have the computer and information on the information utilities you want to use, only two other items are necessary to begin telecomputing: a modem and telecommunications software.

A modem (short for modulator demodulator) takes the signals from your computer and converts them into tones that can be reliably transmitted over phone lines. It also converts tones transmitted to your computer into signals the IBM PC can process.

Your IBM PC does not automatically come with a modem, nor is it ready to be connected to a modem, unless you have the new XT version. There are two common ways to get it connected. First, you can buy a modem on an expansion card and insert it directly into expansion slots in the IBM PC. The expansion slots are connectors inside the main chassis where accessories can be connected. This type of modem generally costs more, but you don't need a serial port to use it with the computer.

Another way of connecting a modem requires a serial port. You can buy an expansion card that has an RS-232 serial interface and then buy an ordinary modem that plugs into the serial port. The XT version has the RS-232 interface built in. IBM and many other companies have expansion cards with a serial interface on them. One of the popular models is the *Asynchronous Communications Adapter* available from most IBM dealers for $120. Other companies sell a serial card for less than that, and many *combo* cards have a serial interface, as well as extra memory, a parallel interface, and other accessories.

If you will need the serial interface for other things like connecting a serial printer to the computer, we suggest you add a modem by installing a serial interface and then connecting a standard modem to it.

Modems

Modems for the IBM PC come with a wide variety of different features having to do with how the modem hooks to your computer and how it hooks to the telephone line. Modems that install directly in your computer are generally more expensive than those that require a serial port. Modems are also available in *acoustic* and *direct-connect* models. Acoustic modems connect to the telephone through rubber cups in which the telephone handset is placed. Direct-connect modems can be plugged directly into a telephone jack. We prefer direct-connect modems because they operate more reliably. Some modems have special features, like the ability to dial telephone numbers. Some will even transmit messages for you, such as your account number and any information the utility needs to get you signed on. In addition, modems transmit data at different speeds. Most information services will work fine with a modem that transmits at 300 BAUD or bits per second (BPS). Some services also work with faster, 1200 BPS, modems. Since you generally pay for services by the minute, a modem that transmits and receives data at a faster rate may save money in the long run. As you might expect, modems that can transmit at 1200 BPS cost more than 300 BPS modems.

Two popular modems that insert directly into the expansion slots of the IBM PC are:

- *BIZCOMP 2120 PC:IntelliModem*. This is a complete telecommunications package. It consists of an expansion card that plugs into the computer, the necessary cables to connect you to the telephone line, and a complete instruction manual. This package is sold by Business Computer Corporation for $499.
- *PC Modem Plus*. This modem system is similar to The BIZCOMP version but has one major feature that may be desirable. With this modem, you can use a variety of telecommunications software. You aren't restricted to the software that comes with the modem. The PC Modem Plus is sold by Ven-Tel, Inc., for $749.

There are many different modems that connect to the serial card. Here are some that are popular among IBM PC owners:

- *Hayes Stack Smartmodem* from Hayes Microcomputer Products Co. sells for $699. It connects straight into an RS-232 card and then into the telephone line. This modem can automatically dial a number, answer the phone, and change from send to receive modes by itself. It is popular because it is so easy to use.

• A whole series of modems called *Cat Modems* is sold by Novation. These modems give reliable service and are available through most computer stores. You can buy a Cat Modem for as little as $149 or as much as $695. The *212 Auto-Cat Modem* is the $695 version. This modem has both automatic answering and automatic dialing capabilities and can operate at both 300 and 1200 BPS. It is a reliable, good looking modem that is widely available.

• The *Microconnection* marketed by The Microperipheral Corporation connects directly into a telephone line and has automatic dialing. This modem can run a printer and keep track of incoming information from different telephone lines. The price is $225.

• Radio Shack sells a complete line of modems priced from $150 to over $500. If you want a simple, no-frills modem, the inexpensive models from Radio Shack are good buys and work reliably.

Software for Telecommunications

A critical portion of your telecommunications system is a software package that tells the IBM PC computer how to send and receive information. Most of the modems that connect directly to the IBM PC come with their own software for telecommunications (called terminal software). All telecommunications software will transmit material you type on the keyboard to the modem and display data received from the modem on the screen. Sophisticated software may do much more, such as store incoming information on a disk, print incoming or outgoing data on a printer, transmit material from a file on a disk to another computer, and automatically dial the phone. Here are a few of the many telecommunications programs for the PC.

The *Asynchronous Communications Support* is a reliable product that will just do the basics. It is available from IBM for $40.

The *Smart Term/PC* from Persoft ($150) does a lot more. You can save, transfer, and print out information, and you can download programs. This program will even answer your phone when you aren't at home, and transmit and receive data. It comes in several versions that emulate the operation of popular terminals from Digital Equipment Corporation. A terminal is a keyboard/display device that lets you communicate with a remotely located computer over phone lines. This software lets the IBM PC work as if it were a DEC terminal. It works with a variety of modems.

Another sophisticated terminal program for the PC is *Microterm* sold by Micro-Systems Software. It lets you transfer files to another computer over the phone, and it can be set up to automatically dial, connect to, and transmit files to another computer at any time. Thus, you could set up *Microterm* before going to bed and let it transmit an important file to another computer in the middle of the night when rates are lower. *Microterm* also lets you assign phrases to keys so that frequently used phrases (for example, the material you type in

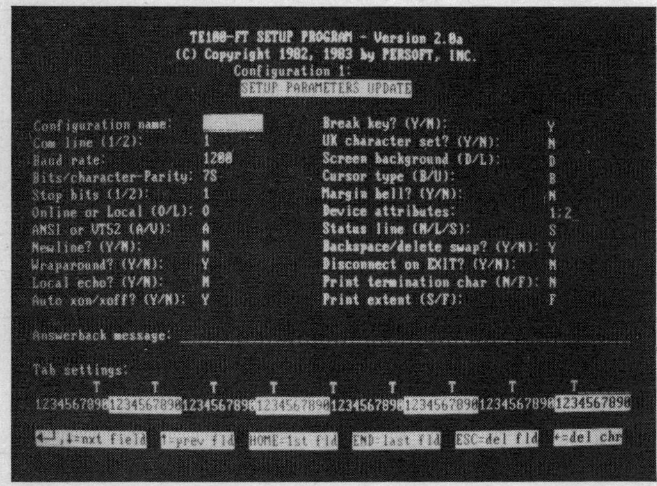

Figure 6.1   Smart Term/PC

when signing on to an information utility) are transmitted with one key press. *Microterm* is $79.95.

The final telecommunications program for the PC to be discussed here is the *Peachware Telecommunications* program from Peachtree Software. This program certainly gets the nod for the nicest looking documentation. It comes with a boxed set of documentation in a soft vinyl binder. *Peachware Telecommunications* is more than a pretty box, however. It also has automatic dialing; it can store incoming data in a disk file and transmit data from a disk file. This program can also automatically respond to a call and connect the computer to the phone line. It works with many popular modems and has a well organized, informative manual. It is $150.

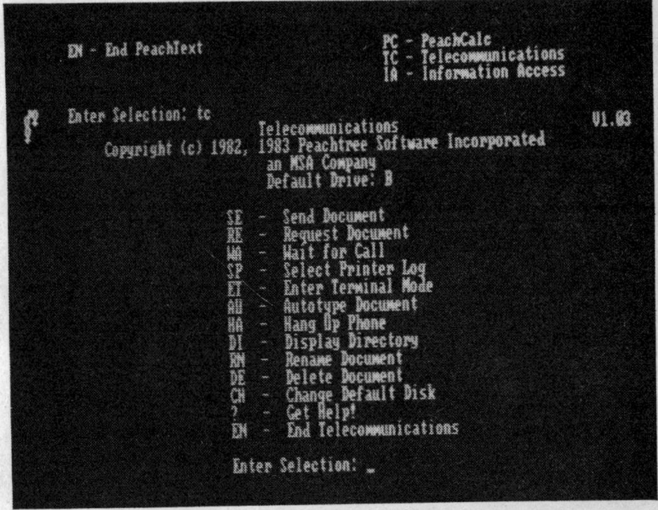

Figure 6.2   Peachware Telecommunications

CHAPTER SEVEN

Word Processing

WHAT IS WORD PROCESSING?

When you think of a computer, you may think of numbers, numbers, and more numbers. Are computers *number crunchers*, machines capable of performing thousands of calculations a second? Yes, they are, and the next chapter on business and professional applications deals with the ability of the computer to manipulate and massage all sorts of numbers for you.

Computers are also for word people. We feel that computers, particularly personal computers, may well turn out to do more work with words than with numbers. The chapter on telecommunications showed you how to harness the power of the computer to acquire and communicate information. That is called *information processing*. This chapter focuses on the role of the computer in helping you create written documents— from a quick note to the folks back East to that great American novel you always wanted to write. Using a computer to write your own material is called *word processing*.

WHY USE A WORD PROCESSOR?

If you are an accomplished typist and own a typewriter, why should you learn to use a word processor? If you type documents that are used only once, and you always type them perfectly, you have little reason to learn word processing. If you make errors, if you find yourself typing the same thing several times (for example, a letter that is to be mailed to several people), or if you must regularly revise and retype documents, a word processor can help you do more work in less time.

A friend of ours is the chairman of a scholarship committee that awards eight college scholarships each year and receives between 50 and 150 applications. Each year he must send out eight letters congratulating those who received the awards, eight letters to the alternates who might still get the award if some of the first eight decide not to attend college, and a larger number of letters to the people who were turned down. He has three standard letters that he modifies slightly each year. Before he began using the word processor, he or his secretary had to type each letter, check it for errors, retype it if errors were found, and finally sign and mail each one. With a word processor, he tells the program to load the file containing the standard letter into the computer's memory, the computer displays the letter on the screen, and he edits it to reflect circumstances related to the current year's competition, adding any personal messages he wants. Then he types the correct address at the top of the letter (actually at the top of the screen) and presses the keys to tell the computer to print out a copy on a *letter quality* printer. (A letter quality printer has print that looks as good as that produced by a standard office typewriter.)

Once the current version of the letter is in the computer's memory, he only needs to add the address and salutation and individual comments. If eighty percent of the letter remains the same, that part need not be retyped for each person who receives the letter. This means he doesn't waste time typing the same thing over and over, and he doesn't increase the likelihood of making a typing error by retyping material that has already been typed correctly.

As our friend adds comments and the address to the standard letter, he occasionally makes a mistake. On a typewriter he would have to stop and correct the error. If the typewriter is a self-correcting model, it is sometimes possible to make the correction cleanly and quickly. But if he leaves out a line or wants to add a word in the middle of a sentence, he has to retype the entire letter. With virtually all word processing programs you can *insert* and *delete* material electronically. If you typed *Tkhis* when you wanted *This*, it is very easy to use the cursor control keys (the ones with the arrows on them) to move the cursor over the top of the *k* in *Tkhis*. You press the DEL key, and the *k* disappears. In addition, the word processor fills in the space. Instead of *T his* you have *This*. Most word processors let you delete material a character at a time, some allow deletion of words, sentences, even paragraphs by pressing one or two keys. The insert function works much like the delete function. If you type *Your application was one of the best* and then decide that you want to add the word *very* after *the*, it is a simple matter for a word processor. Move the cursor to the space just after *the* and press the INSERT key. Most word processors then create a *window* at that point on the screen, and you can type in anything you want. When you've finished, you press INSERT again, and the window closes around the new material. On a typewriter you would have to type the entire letter again.

We find the ability to insert and delete material electronically does more than speed up the writing process. Because the process of editing and changing material is difficult on a type-writer, our manuscripts gradually turned into a mass of red pencil marks. Eventually the draft became unusable because it was difficult to follow all the changes and corrections. In addition, we often rejected the idea of going through another draft, and retyping the document yet another time, because of the time it took. With a word processor, corrections occur as you make them. There is no need to have the document retyped to see how it reads with revisions. If you want to move a paragraph from page 2 to the middle of page 8, most programs let you mark that paragraph and tell the computer to transfer it electronically to a new location. You make insertions, dele-tions, and block moves with a few keystrokes, and you see the result of your editing immediately. Some programs even have an *undo* command that lets you go back to the way the doc-ument was before the last change, just in case you decide it was better before. We are able to do our revisions more quickly, and we can do more of them because the boring manual labor has been reduced. Now we can concentrate on the editing process rather than worrying about having the time to retype that report yet another time. A sentence that was typed correctly the first time need never be retyped, even if the document goes through many revisions! What takes only a few minutes on the word processor would take hours with a typewriter.

WHAT MAKES A GOOD WORD PROCESSING COMPUTER?

Large Capacity Screen Display. The more you can see on the screen at once the easier it is to compose and edit your document. An excellent word processor has at least a 24-line by 80-character display. In addition, it would be nice to be able to duplicate on the screen the effect of special printing codes that underline or print words in bold.

The PC has a very good 24-by-80 character display. One word of caution though: word processing is much easier on your eyes if you use a non-color (monochrome) monitor. Color monitors, when used with the IBM PC, tend to distort the letters slightly, causing more eye strain. The standard monochrome monitor sold by IBM is excellent for word processing.

A Keyboard with Many Function Keys. The keyboard is another important thing to look at when you evaluate the word processing potential of a computer. In our opinion, a standard typewriter keyboard is absolutely essential. Some keyboards have small keyboards that are unacceptable for word processing. It's true that you can get accustomed to just about anything, but like a rock in your shoe, a non-standard keyboard is something you may never feel good about. The IBM PC has a standard keyboard with some of the keys in the wrong place.

We have several complaints about the IBM keyboard. There is a long-standing debate in word processing circles about whether the ideal word processing machine should have many keys or only a few keys. If there are many keys, then many word processing features can have a specific, labeled key. For example, there can be a key marked SAVE. When you want to save a file you have created, you can simply push that key. If you only have the standard letter and number keys, then you will have to memorize a set of directions. SAVE may require you to type an S, for example. Also, you will probably have to push more than one key at a time to use many features of the program. For instance, to insert a line, you may have to hold down the CONTROL key while you strike the S key.

The IBM PC has 82 keys, not counting the space bar. This is more than some and fewer than others. One IBM look-a-like, the Eagle PC has 104 keys, not counting the space bar! Compare both these machines with the TRS-80 Model 4, which has only 69 keys. The PC has many special purpose keys but not as many as some of its competitors.

Our real complaint has to do with the design of the keyboard. The shift keys are small, hard to find, and misplaced. The RETURN key is placed about one row too high. If you are a good typist, this keyboard will drive you mad. We feel that the standard for all keyboards should be the IBM Selectric typewriter. It seems ironic that IBM didn't adopt its keyboard format for their computer. Fortunately, a lot of hardware companies have recognized the problem. You can buy a standard Selectric-style keyboard for about $200 from Keytronic and others.

Fast, High-Capacity, Reliable Mass Storage. Professional word processing calls for reliable, high-capacity mass storage. The least expensive version of the PC does not have a disk drive, but you can use a cassette storage system. We would advise against using word processors with cassette systems. You can get the IBM PC in a one-disk or two-disk version, however, and a hard disk system (the XT) is also available. The high-capacity drives store about 360K on each disk and are reliable. If you want to do a lot of word processing, you might want to get the ten-million-character hard disk drive. It will store over 20,000 copies of this book.

Plenty of RAM. This may or may not be an issue for you. If you type material no longer than a typical business letter, you will not need lots of memory to hold the document as you type it in. However, if you type term papers, reports, magazine articles or books, you will find it very inconvenient to work on a computer with limited RAM. On this point, the IBM PC gets high marks. The standard IBM PC has 128K RAM and can be expanded to 512K. Our first four books were written on a computer with 32K of memory. You can do lots of work with very little memory, but it is not as convenient and errors are more likely to occur.

Freedom from Glitchitis. Glitchitis is a disease commonly found in all sorts of electronic equipment. It generally strikes when a malfunction will do the most damage. It frequently occurs for no known cause and cannot be duplicated when you try to figure out just what happened. Worse yet, it is least likely to happen when you are trying to explain the problem to someone who can fix it. Duplication is possible, if you use the computer again for an important task (like typing the term paper at 1:00 a.m. that is due at 9:00 A.M.). The IBM PC is remarkably free of the glitchitis disease, although some of its competitors are prone to it.

DESIRABLE WORD PROCESSING FEATURES

Hundreds of word processors are available for small computers. Prices start at about $30 and go up to well over $1000. Programs for the IBM PC are generally priced in the high end of that range. There are a lot of new or revised programs coming on the market all the time. By the time you read this, there may be many good programs not even mentioned here. For this reason we will give you a brief checklist of features to look for in a word processor. This is not an exhaustive list, but it will alert you to many of the features commonly available.

Delete Modes

This refers to ways you can delete text from the screen. Some simple programs permit nothing more than deleting material a character at a time. Others have many options. Here are the common options:

- Delete character.
- Delete word—Deletes material separated by spaces on each end.
- Delete sentence—Deletes material from a capital letter preceded by a space to a period or other end punctuation.
- Delete line—Deletes a line of text on the screen. A poor substitute for delete sentence, since lines on the screen rarely correspond with sentence length.
- Delete partial line—Deletes from cursor to end of line, for example.
- Delete paragraph—Deletes from beginning of indented sentence to beginning of another indented sentence.
- Delete block—See section on blocks for explanation.
- Delete everything—Deletes everything in the memory of the computer.
- Delete undo—Save me from the error of my ways, because I didn't really mean to do that.
- Delete verify—If instructed to delete a lot of material, the program checks (it asks REALLY Y/N? or PRESS RETURN TO DELETE DOCUMENT) before executing the instruction.

Insert Modes

This refers to the methods available to add or insert material in an existing document.

- Destructive insert—Replaces material by typing over it.
- Non-destructive insert—Pushes material out of the way as new material is typed in or creates a *window* of blank space where new material can be typed.

Block Modes

A block is a section of text you have marked electronically. You might press the down arrow key at the beginning of a section and press it again at the end of that section. The computer can then be told to perform different operations on that block of text. Blocks of text can be moved, deleted, or duplicated. Duplicating a block means you can put the same material in several places in the text. Reports often contain many complicated tables that have the same format but different numbers. A complicated table can be typed once, marked as a block of text, and inserted at any point in the text where you want the table. Once you have the table in place, all you have to do is fill in the numbers.

- Delete block—Can a block be deleted?
- Move block—Can a block be moved from one location to another?
- Duplicate block—Can a block be duplicated somewhere else in the document without erasing it from its original location?
- Multiple block—Can more than one block be marked, or is the program limited to one marked block at a time?

Cursor Control

The cursor is a solid or blinking rectangle that tells you where material you type will appear on the screen. It also tells you what will be affected by an instruction to insert or delete material. For example, you must move the cursor over a letter to delete it in most programs. Simple word processing programs let you control cursor movement with arrow keys that point in the direction the cursor will move. On the IBM PC, most programs use the cursor keys on the numeric keypad.

- Move by character—The cursor moves one character at a time.
- Move by character, auto repeat—Hold down a key, and the cursor keeps going until you release the key.
- Move by word—The cursor moves to the first letter in the next word.
- Move by sentence—The cursor moves to first letter after an ending punctuation mark.

• Move by paragraph—The cursor moves to beginning of next paragraph.

• End/beginning of line—The cursor moves to end or beginning of line.

• Home—The cursor moves to home position, the top left corner of screen.

• Beginning—The cursor moves to beginning of document.

• End—The cursor moves to end of document.

• Fast scroll—The cursor jumps forward or backward in document several lines at a time.

Search and Replace

If you misspell a word throughout a document, can you tell the computer to find and correct the error? If you have a large document in memory, can you find a particular section by telling the computer to search for a particular word or phrase? There are several variations on the search and replace theme:

• Search for keyword—Looks for a word you specify and moves the cursor to the point where it occurs.

• Replace, once—Finds the target word and replaces it with a new word you specify.

• Selective replace—Finds the target word and asks if you want it changed to the new word specified. You can say yes or no.

• Global replace—Finds multiple occurrences of the target word and changes them to the replacement word you specify.

• Selective global replace—Same as selective replace but checks entire document.

• Wild card search—Lets you specify the target word with *wild card* letters. Telling it to search for Th#mes, for example, means words like Themes and Thames would be found, because the third letter is a wild card; any letter is acceptable in that position.

Page and Printing Features

• Programmable page parameters—Can the number of lines, the number of characters on a line, and the amount of space left at the top and bottom margins be controlled?

• Printer selection—Will the program work with many different types of printers, or is it limited to only one or two?

• Underline—Will it produce underlined text?

• Boldface—Will it produce boldfaced text?

• Large characters—Will it produce expanded or larger-than-normal characters on printers that support such an option?

• Italics—Will it produce italicized print on printers that support that option?

• Justification—will it print justified text, with the right- and left-hand margins even?

• Sub/superscripts—Does it support subscripts and super-scripts?

• Headers and footers—Will the program let you specify a message that will appear at the top or bottom of each page?

• Page numbering—Will the program automatically number pages for you?

• See/get—Will the program show you on the screen what you will get when the document is printed?

• Wraparound—Will the program automatically move to the next line when you run out of room on the current line? Does it take the word you are typing and move it down to the next line, or does it break the word and leave parts of it on different lines? Breaking words up is a poor substitute for true wraparound that automatically moves the last word typed on a line, the one that is too long to fit, to the beginning of the next line.

Some of the word processors for the IBM PC have most of these and many more. This list gives you a starting point from which to evaluate word processors. You may also want to consider two other types of programs. There are programs that look at each word in a document and check spelling. These programs won't tell you if you used *effective* when you really needed *affective*. Both *effective* and *affective* are correctly spelled words and will be accepted by a spelling checker. Words like *affeccived* or *therr* will be caught, however, by the checker. There is also a program called *Grammatik* that checks grammar and may even make suggestions for improving your writing.

What Word Processing
Programs are Available?

There are many different word processing programs available for the IBM PC. These programs range in price from around $50 to more than $500. If we reviewed all the programs in this book, there would be space for nothing else. We will describe only a few of the more popular programs.

You might also be interested in two articles about word processing. *InfoWorld Magazine* published an article entitled "InfoWorld's Guide to Word-Processing Programs" (Vol. 5, No. 3, p. 27). This article discusses scores of different word processing programs. Another good article appeared in *Personal Computing* in April 1983 (p. 110). It's entitled "Word Processing: Finding the Right Software."

WordStar

The best-known word processing program is MicroPro's *WordStar*. The suggested retail price is $495. Like all other programs, this one has strengths and weaknesses. As you might guess from the price, this program is extremely powerful and has many features. This is wonderful for some people and terrible for others. The program has so many features it is difficult to learn Band use. In addition, the documentation that comes with it is terrible. It's at its best in an office where there is someone who can become an expert. This is NOT a program for occasional users. Unless you have extensive word processing needs, you'll probably not want to buy *WordStar*. Even then, you may want to look at several other programs before selecting *WordStar*.

WordStar has most of the features you would expect in an expensive word processing package. It features automatic text justification, automatic indentation, the ability to edit and print at the same time, and a display that shows you where each page will end when you print your document. The screen will display *almost* exactly what the printout looks like, except underlining and boldfacing. All the standard editing features are present, including insertions, deletions, and block manipulations.

There are many compatible add-on programs. *MailMerge* ($250), *SpellStar* ($250), and *StarIndex* ($195) are also available from MicroPro. These programs personalize form letters, correct spelling, and create indexes. *InfoStar* ($495) and *CalcStar* ($195) automatically insert business data and financial projections into *WordStar* documents.

After all this, you might think *WordStar* is the perfect word processor. It isn't. No program is best for everyone. *WordStar* has many features, but what if you don't need many features? Then its complexity becomes an albatross around your neck instead of an inevitable accompaniment to flexibility.

Then, too, if you buy a word processing program with more features than you need, you not only waste money, you waste memory. *WordStar* is a great example of that. *WordStar* takes up a lot of memory. With *WordStar* in memory, there is room for only about ten pages of a document in RAM, in a system with a minimum amount of memory. If your document is longer than ten pages, *WordStar* can handle it, but only by going back and forth to the disk for portions stored there. This can result in a ten-second delay if you are moving from page to page.

Aha, you say. *I'll get around that problem. I'll load up my IBM with a super big memory!* Sorry. *WordStar* can use only 64K of memory at one time, no matter how much memory you've added. This is a glaring deficiency, in our opinion.

WordStar also has other problems. Like most word processors, you can order the program to search for all occurrences of a given string of text. Unfortunately, the program will overlook the string if part of it appears on one line and the rest on another line.

Another problem relates to software support. In the past, MicroPro has not been very helpful when contacted about *WordStar* problems.

Spellbinder

Spellbinder (Lexisoft) is another multi-feature word processing program designed to compete with programs like *WordStar*. This program also sells for $495. *Spellbinder* seems to have been intended to do everything that *WordStar* would do, and yet be easier to learn. The manual is a lot better than the one that comes with *WordStar*, but it lacks one extremely important feature: an index. We find that to be almost a fatal error in documenting any software. Indexes are essential if you're looking for ease of use. This weakness could be easily rectified, since the manual is good otherwise. It has a tutorial, as well as a quick reference section and a general reference section.

The program gives all the expected features in a top-of-the-line word processor. It even includes the ability to custom-design other features by using what amounts to a language called *M-Speak*. It also gives user-definable keys, sorting of customer records by nineteen classifications, alphabetizing by name, zip code sorting, and the ability to merge a list of customer records into a form letter so the letter looks individually prepared. Two-column printing is possible. There is a function that will print several different files in one batch. Math functions such as column and row additions and fixed point arithmetic are also available.

Overall the program is as good as *WordStar* and is much easier to learn. It has one very serious flaw, though. It can only use 128K of memory. The program itself takes up 100K of memory. This means that a chapter the length of this one will not fit in the computer. You either have to break it into two pieces or use a complicated command routine. This is a limitation of the *program*, not your computer. If you have

256K of memory, the program still only uses 128K. This may not be a serious limitation if you never write long documents, but it seems an unnecessary limitation to us.

The Final Word

The Final Word is a new word processing program from Mark of the Unicorn. The suggested retail price for this multi-purpose program is $300. This package features all the standard editing features, plus a unique feature that you can use to view and edit two files simultaneously. The program lets you use a *split screen*, with one document displayed on each of two sections of the screen. You can scroll through one or both documents and move sections from one document to the other.

Another interesting feature of *The Final Word* is that whenever you stop typing for a few seconds, your text is automatically saved on disk. You don't lose the original document, but your new document is saved and protected even if the computer is turned off or the electricity fails.

It's difficult to find a criticism of *The Final Word*. It's complex, of course, just as *WordStar* is, and so the same advice applies here: if you don't need all the features, find something simpler. Another minor criticism is that the bottom two lines of the screen are used for program information. We find that to be distracting and prefer that the top of the screen be used for this purpose. *The Final Word* is an excellent multi-feature word processing program.

EasyWriter

EasyWriter is IBM's contribution to word processing on the IBM PC. The first version of *EasyWriter* met with substantial criticism. IBM went back to the drawing board and has now released version 1.1 of this program. The suggested retail price is $175.

EasyWriter has several things going for it. First, it is easy to learn. Second, the price is significantly lower than the other two word processing programs we have reviewed in this chapter. *EasyWriter* still has some problems, of course. The primary ones are that it is still irritatingly slow, and the maximum document length with 64K of memory is only 14,000 characters. Might these shortcomings be the target of future releases?

By the way, don't confuse this program with one called *EasyWriter II*. This is a totally different, more sophisticated, and more expensive program from another company.

EasyWriter II

EasyWriter II is the newest word processing program from Information Unlimited Software. It is another full-featured but expensive word processor for the IBM PC. In fact, it is one of the most popular. *EasyWriter II* is part of a whole family of programs in the *Easy* series. There is also a spelling checker (*EasySpeller II*), a database management program (*EasyFiler*), an electronic spreadsheet (*EasyPlanner*), and a series of ac-

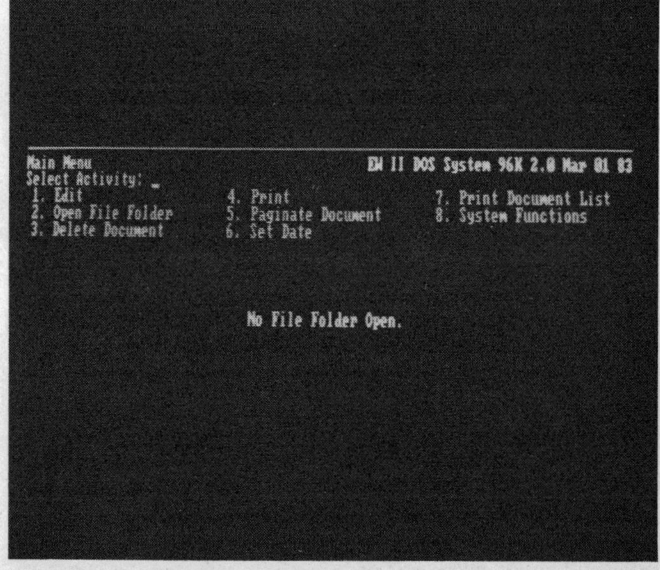

Figure 7.1   Menu from EasyWriter

counting and inventory programs in the *EasyBusiness* series.

With a pricetag of $350, you expect this word processor to be a good one, and it is. All the normal features are available. One of its most attractive features is the *see-get* feature. If you want something printed in boldface, many word processors indicate that on the screen with little symbols before and after the material to be boldfaced. In *EasyWriter II*, you see the material displayed in boldface on the screen. The same goes for underlining. If you will be using page numbers and footers or headers, you even see those on the screen when a page of the document is displayed.

Overall we prefer *EasyWriter II* to *WordStar* and feel it offers as much power but is easier to learn. Some of our friends, however, feel *EasyWriter II* doesn't match *WordStar* in sophistication.

The Benchmark

This $500 program compares favorably with the other expensive word processing programs when it comes to features. Many people feel *The Benchmark* is one of the easier to learn to use of the high-priced word processors. If you need the ultimate in powerful word processing software but want a program that is easy to learn to use, consider *The Benchmark*. Metasoft Corporation, the developer of *The Benchmark*, also has a mailing list program, a spelling checker, and a telecommunications package compatible with *The Benchmark*. The company describes this program as "a serious business tool designed to be used in the most demanding environment—the high production office." We agree.

Volkswriter

Although the advertising for this program makes just as many outlandish claims for its power as all the rest of the word processor ads, we must disagree. *Volkswriter* ($195) is not as powerful as *EasyWriter II* or *WordStar*. However, it is a very useful program that is easy to learn and easy to use. *Volkswriter* has fewer options, fewer ways of doing things like search and replace, inserting text, and moving the cursor.

We're not saying you can't search and replace, insert text, and move the cursor in *Volkswriter*. You can. It's just that you have fewer ways of doing them. Fewer is better for many people who use a word processor occasionally and have a hard time remembering all the complicated instructions that get in your way in an ultrasophisticated word processor.

This is a moderately powerful word processor that makes up in ease of use what it lacks in power.

WordVision

You may have heard of *WordVision* already in publications like the *Wall Street Journal*. The company that developed *WordVision*, Bruce and James, created quite a stir among software publishers when they announced *WordVision* and declared

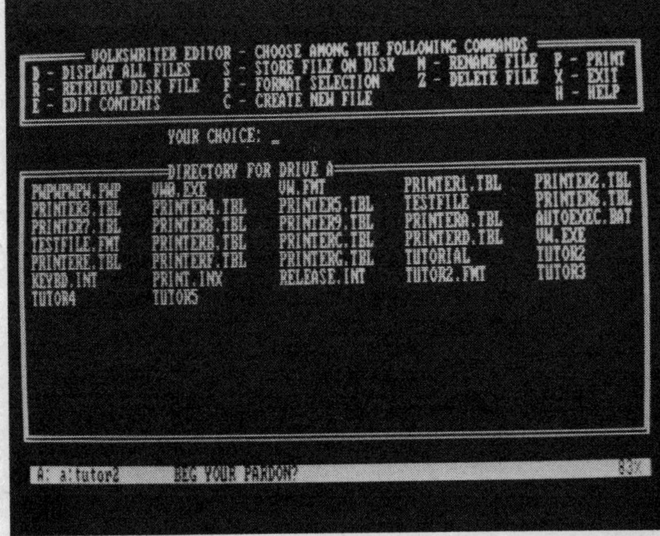

Figure 7.2   Volkswriter: Editor

they would be selling a sophisticated word processing program for the IBM PC for $50. They made headlines again when they signed a lucrative contract with Simon and Schuster to distribute *WordVision* to bookstores and software outlets.

We had an opportunity to work with an early version of *WordVision* before all the bugs had been ironed out. It is quite a word processor for $50. Like *Volkswriter*, it is not as sophisticated as the $500 word processing programs, but it is very easy to use, it comes with a good manual, and it is certainly priced right. If you want an inexpensive, moderately powerful word processing program for the IBM PC, we suggest you consider *WordVision*.

The program is the first in a series of inexpensive programs to be developed by Bruce and James.

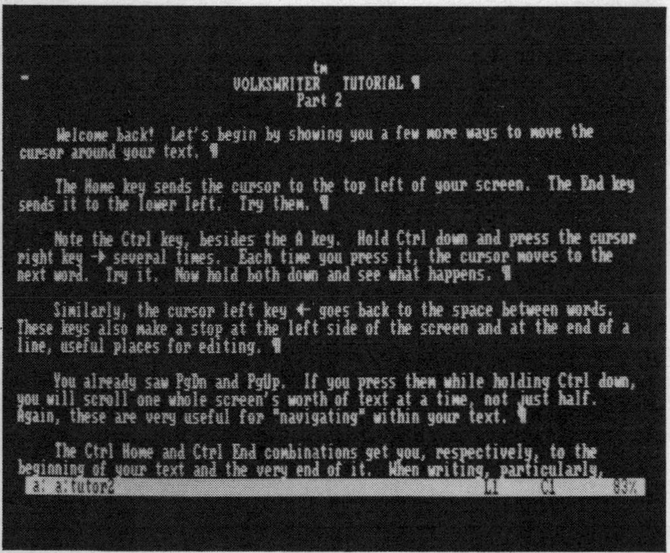

Figure 7.3   Volkswriter: Tutorial

Spelling Checkers Can Aid Word Processing

Spelling checkers are helpful *add-ons* for your word processor. They look through your document and compare your spelling to thousands of words in a built-in spelling dictionary. If you have used a word not listed in the dictionary, the program shows you the word and lets you change it, leave it alone, or enter the word in the dictionary.

Grammar checkers examine your sentence structure and make suggestions for improvements. Some grammar checkers also look for misplaced parentheses, quotation marks, or other incorrect punctuation and even alert you to sexist language.

Grammatik from Aspen Software Co. is an excellent grammar checker for use with the IBM PC. List price for *Grammatik* is $75. *Grammatik* finds more than fifteen kinds of common errors missed by spelling checkers. It analyzes writing style at both the word and sentence level and looks for typographical errors. The program checks for poor or wordy usage, extremely long words and sentences, doubled words and punctuation marks. About 100 gender-specific and possibly sexist words also can be flagged. *Grammatik* finds possible errors, shows them to you in context, and makes suggestions for revision.

Several companies sell spelling checkers that will work with documents written with word processing programs on the IBM PC.

The same company that publishes *Grammatik* also sells *The Random House Proofreader*, a spelling checker listing for $50 and up and based on the *Random House Dictionary*. The number of words included in this spelling checker can be varied according to the memory of your computer. You may choose from 20,000-, 32,000-, 50,000-, or 83,000-word checkers for 55K, 74K, 108K, and 180K systems respectively. The program shows you the error and the sentence it is in. You can correct the mistake, ignore it, accept it, or tell the program to learn it. If you are unsure of the spelling you can call up the dictionary.

Spell-It is another spelling checker for the IBM PC. This program from Berzurk Systems uses a 45,000-word dictionary, finds misspellings, and suggests corrections. The price of *Spell-It* is $29.95.

Both of these spelling checkers are excellent, but they are rather slow. *Spellguard* (Innovative Software Applications) is an extremely fast spelling checker. It reads long manuscripts in just a few seconds. *Spellguard* uses a 20,000-word dictionary and sells for $295.

CHAPTER EIGHT

Business and Professional Applications

If you are thinking about buying a personal computer to help you in business, you came to the right place. The IBM excells as a business tool. Now don't get us wrong. You won't be able to use the PC to manage the affairs of a firm the size of General Motors, but you'll find it helpful in many kinds of business dealings. It is hard at work on the desks of managers in businesses of all sizes, it does all the computing work in many small businesses, and it dutifully does its work for individuals in hundreds of different professions. In fact, most people who buy the IBM PC do so with business applications in mind. With disk drives, a high-capacity display, a full-size keyboard, and the ability to use over half a million bytes of memory, the IBM PC is an excellent machine for professional and business uses.

The PC can computerize routine accounting tasks. For example, Peachtree Software has a complete set of accounting software programs for the IBM PC. You can buy General Ledger, Accounts Receivable, and Accounts Payable programs in a special *Peachpak* that costs $395. Peachtree Software is one of the leading producers of business software and also sells programs for inventory management, word processing, telecommunications, and more. Another set of accounting programs is the *Accounting Plus* series from Software Dimensions. This set includes software for general ledger, accounts payable, accounts receivable, inventory control, purchase order, payroll, and sales order management. If you are interested in accounting software for the IBM PC, we suggest you write Peachtree Software and Software Dimensions for catalogs. Both

**Figure 8.1   An IBM Personal Computer
is useful to professional workers.**

companies provide extensive descriptions of their business programs.

Although the use of the IBM PC for accounting is widespread, the most common use is as a managerial tool. We will concentrate on that aspect in this chapter. Telecommunications and word processing will be of interest to many business and professional people. People in management roles must also deal with planning, so we'll start out by talking about ways the computer can help you with that task.

If you want to use your computer for planning, your main concern is projections. You want the answers to questions such as "What will happen if sales increase by ten percent?" The answers to many questions beginning with *What if* can help you make decisions about the future. One type of program that helps answer *what if* questions is an electronic spreadsheet.

Spreadsheets

Accountants and others who analyze finances have been using spreadsheets for a long time. A spreadsheet is simply a rectangular worksheet using rows and columns of numbers.

This form is used because it keeps the numbers organized. A column of numbers with a total is a simple spreadsheet. Now what happens when a number is changed? The total for that column is wrong! If you are doing your work by hand, and you change several numbers in several columns, you have to recalculate all the totals. The larger the number of rows and columns on the worksheet, the more complicated it becomes to change any one number. Imagine how many hours of work would be involved in changing and updating a complicated financial forecast.

A spreadsheet analysis done without a computer is tedious. You can avoid much of this tedium by using your IBM PC and an electronic spreadsheet. There are now a variety of electronic spreadsheets available for the IBM computer and for almost every other small computer.

VisiCalc

VisiCalc was the first electronic spreadsheet program for personal computers. It has been so successful that many other companies now produce electronic spreadsheet programs. Today there are more than sixty different electronic spreadsheets available for small computers!

VisiCalc has been such a success because it cuts down on the amount of work you must do when you use a spreadsheet. In fact, if you have *VisiCalc*, most of what you have to do is to get the numbers and information into the computer. After that, simple commands can tell the computer to rearrange the information in almost any way you want. With *VisiCalc* you can:

- Get the total of the values of any series of locations, for example, all of top row or all of the first column.
- Get the average for any series of numbers.
- Try different values on your data to get projections.
- See certain data organized in a graph and then print it.

Assume that you are a district sales manager for a large company. You have been asked to prepare a sales estimate for next fiscal year that gives three different levels of performance. You supervise twenty-five sales representatives, your company has 350 products ranging in price from $3.95 to $225, and you have nineteen different discount plans. Your regional manager wants your sales estimate by next week, and you just found out about it today. If you do the work by hand, it could take days, and you don't have days. Believe it or not, you could probably do this complicated sales analysis in just a single afternoon with *VisiCalc*.

How does *VisiCalc* do all this? Your computer screen becomes a window showing you a certain section of a giant spreadsheet made up of 254 rows and 64 columns. You can move this window around simply by using the arrow keys on the computer to view any portion of the spreadsheet you desire. When you want to make comparisons, the screen can even be split so you can see two different parts of the spreadsheet at one time. You can ask the computer to search for certain kinds of information, do some calculations, and show you the result.

Once you have entered a formula, you never have to enter it again. You can copy formulas, headings (or titles), and numbers into as many columns as you want. Using our sales estimate as an example, suppose you want to show what would happen if ten of the sales reps had a twenty-five percent increase and all the others had a five percent decrease. All you have to do is tell the computer to multiply your first results by either twenty-five percent or minus five percent wherever appropriate. The computer performs all of the calculations.

Don't get us wrong, though. A program that will do as

much for you as *VisiCalc* will take time to learn to use properly. But if you have to do any kind of financial projections, your time and effort will be well spent. *VisiCalc* is available from VisiCorp for $250.

Programs to Supplement VisiCalc

· There are a great many programs intended to add capabilities to *VisiCalc*. There is no way we can tell you about all these supplemental programs, but we can give you a thumbnail sketch of a representative few. You must have *VisiCalc* to use these programs.

32 VisiCalc Worksheets (dilithium Press) is 34 specific examples of *VisiCalc* in action (there are two *bonus* programs). This package has a disk that can be used with the *VisiCalc* program, and a 175-page book. It costs $34.95 and should be a great help in getting *VisiCalc* working for you. The worksheets are divided into five chapters: Games and

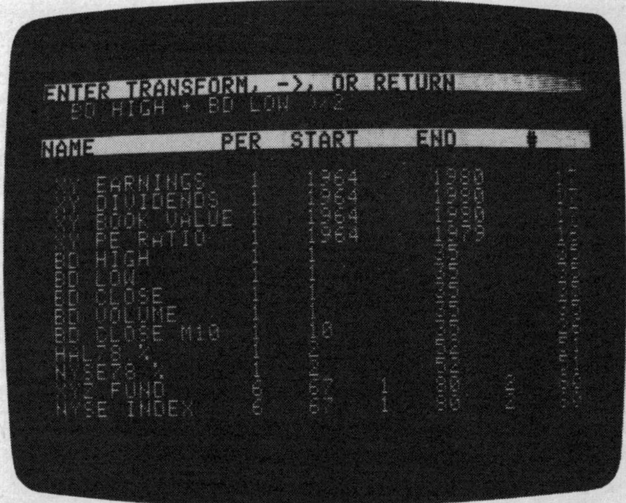

Figure 8.2   VisiTrend/VisiPlot

Novelties (5), Business Applications (10), Household Applications (8), Statistical Analysis (6), and What If Models (5). The business applications include a depreciation schedule, a payroll program, a monthly rental income record, and seven others. We think the most interesting program is one called *Econ* that explores the cause and effect of money flow in the national economy. Supplemental programs like this set let you use the power and convenience of *VisiCalc* without customizing *VisiCalc* for your own particular applications.

VIZ-A-CON (Abacus Associates) is a disk program that supplements *VisiCalc*. *VIZ-A-CON* sells for $139.95 and is designed primarily to make it easier to consolidate data. With it you can *roll up* days into weeks, weeks into months, departments into divisions, divisions into companies, or do any other consolidation of *VisiCalc* data. In addition, a custom formatting feature turns *VisiCalc* into a report writer.

VisiTrend/Plot (VisiCorp) is a handy program for calculating business statistics and for printing out graphs and charts from data generated by *VisiCalc*. It sells for $300 and works with Epson MX-80 and MX-100 and a few other printers. This is a complex program that is probably best tackled after you are very familiar with *VisiCalc*.

Solutions, Inc., produces three software packages designed to let you do some special things with *VisiCalc*: *VIS\Bridge/REPORT*, *VIS\Bridge/SORT*, and *VIS\Bridge/DJ*.

VIS\Bridge/REPORT produces reports that you can tailor yourself. You aren't bound by the page length and width restrictions of *VisiCalc*. You can rearrange the material you have in your *VisiCalc* files and print it out in a report format that suits your needs at the time. This package sells for $79.

VIS\Bridge/SORT sorts the material in your *VisiCalc* files. You can sort the rows or columns of your spreadsheet into either ascending or descending sequences. You can sort on either alphabetic or numeric items. You can use five columns or rows as sort keys. Partial spreadsheets may be sorted while headings and totals remain in place. The price of the software is $89.

VIS\Bridge/DJ loads up-to-date financial information from

the Dow Jones News/Retrieval telecommunications system directly into *VisiCalc*. You can use this to update your business forecasts based on the latest stock market information. This program sells for $259.

StretchCalc (Multisoft Corporation) is another *VisiCalc* supplemental program that adds many new features to *VisiCalc*. For example, you can use *StretchCalc* to generate many types of graphs from data in a *VisiCalc* spreadsheet. It can also be used to sort and organize data in ways not possible with *VisiCalc* alone. The program costs $99.

Taxplanner (QED Software) is a $50 package that helps you evaluate the tax implications of various decisions related to investments and income options. The program includes *VisiCalc* templates that let you enter data from federal and state income tax forms from previous years and then enter additional data to determine the effect of things like real estate purchases, interest expenses, stock sales, and oil and gas investments.

SuperCalc

SuperCalc, produced by Sorcim for $295, is similar to *VisiCalc*. Both spreadsheets have 254 rows and 64 columns, many of the commands are the same, and both spreadsheets are excellent.

There are some important differences. *SuperCalc* has a few more commands than *VisiCalc* and thus is a bit more powerful. *SuperCalc* can also display data in color, but the use of color seems to slow the program down. In general, *SuperCalc* seems to be a little faster, but *VisiCalc* is easier to use. *SuperCalc* gives you a few more options, but *VisiCalc*'s manual is better.

Which spreadsheet is best? This depends on you and what you're going to use it for. If you are planning on purchasing one or the other, there is an excellent magazine article you may want to consult. "Calc Wars" by Andrew Fluegelman appeared in the August 1982 issue of *PC Magazine*. This article does a great job of comparing *SuperCalc* and *VisiCalc*.

How to Use SuperCalc

How to Use SuperCalc (dilithium Software) replaces the manual that comes with the *SuperCalc* program. It is also a guide to application and implementation of spreadsheet programs. Included in the $39.95 purchase price is a disk using the worksheets listed in the book. The book alone is available for $19.95.

Multiplan

Multiplan is another strong contender for supremacy in the IBM *Calc Wars*. Microsoft sells it for $250. It has some capabilities not found in the other two spreadsheets. Most of these are somewhat esoteric and probably won't mean much to you unless your uses are very complicated and sophisticated. For example, in *Multiplan* you can center data within a column while the other two spreadsheets put data flush left or flush right. For most applications it won't make that much differ-

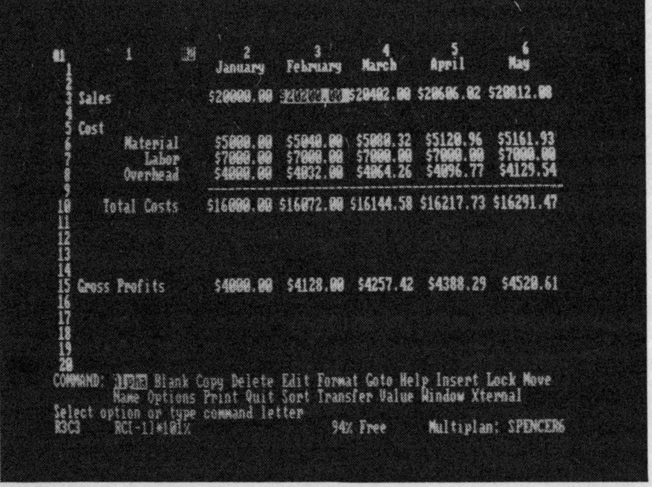

Figure 8.3   Multiplan

ence. There are some real and important differences between *Multiplan* and the other spreadsheets, however. If you would like a detailed analysis of differences between the major electronic spreadsheets, you can read *Spreadsheet Software: From VisiCalc to 1-2-3*, a 336-page book published by Que Corporation.

In general, it is probably accurate to say that *Multiplan* has a few more features, but that is a bit more complicated than *VisiCalc* or *SuperCalc*. This might have some implications for beginners. *Multiplan* might not be the best choice for you if you have had no experience with electronic spreadsheets.

By now you have probably gathered that all three of the electronic worksheets discussed so far in this chapter are very good. They are so nearly equal that we're sure no one would be wise to drop one and switch to another. As far as deciding to buy in the first place, that would be tough. About all we can say is that you should view each in action and experiment with them all. An easy way to evaluate all three programs is to buy a book on each one. It makes more sense to make a $20 mistake on a book rather than a $300 mistake on a program that doesn't fit your needs. If you have a specific application in mind, there may be an add-on product that fits your needs for one or more of the programs, and that may tip the scales.

Programs to Supplement SuperCalc and Multiplan

Financial Planning for Multiplan and the IBM PC (Howard W. Sams) is an $89.95 package of software that works with *Multiplan* on the IBM PC. It contains the templates (the electronic equivalent of blank forms) for many different jobs, such as calculating net present value, internal rate of return, break-even analysis, several mortgage analyzers, and much more. The program makes it very easy to work with these commonly used calculations.

Real Estate Overlays and *Financial Overlays* for *Multiplan* or *SuperCalc* are two packages from RealData. Each package costs around $100 for the IBM PC. Like the program from

Howard W. Sams, these packages are templates that let you use *Multiplan* or *SuperCalc* for special jobs in your area of interest. The *Real Estate Overlays*, for example, help you do calculations related to buying income property: analyzing depreciation options, developing cash flow evaluations, evaluating internal rate of return figures, and producing annual income-and-expense statements, as well as mortgage amortization schedules.

Figure 8.4   Lotus has developed a template for the programmable function keys.

Other Spreadsheet Programs

CalcStar

CalcStar ($195) is sold by MicroPro, the company that publishes the best-selling word processing program called *WordStar*. *CalcStar* does not have as many special features as the more expensive programs, and it is a little slower than other programs, but it is very easy to learn to use. Ease of use and the low cost compared to other spreadsheets make this program attractive.

Report Manager

Report Manager is advertised as a three-dimensional, programmable spreadsheet. Although the title is a little misleading, this is a good package. The third dimension is actually the ability to display data by page. *Report Manager* ($399)

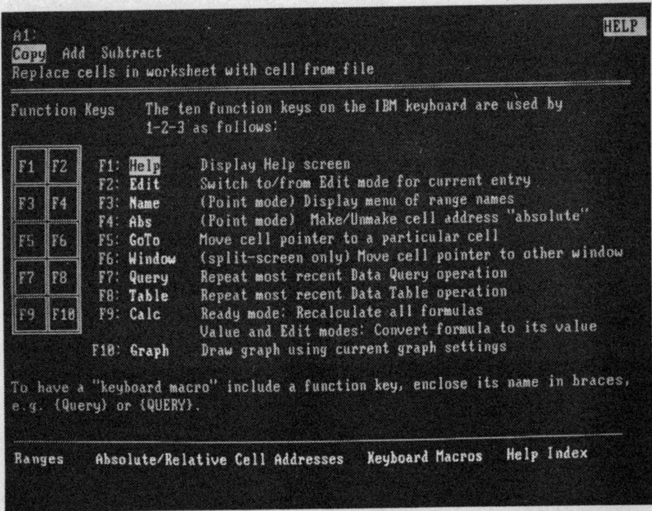

Figure 8.5   1–2–3

will also display data by the two traditional dimensions of rows and columns. This makes it possible, for example, to produce a yearly sales forecast (by month) in two dimensions on one page. Other pages can be devoted to other years.

Integrated Worksheets

As we have mentioned before, there are many other electronic worksheets for the IBM. The competition is fierce, and the *Calc Wars* are just beginning. This intense competition has spawned a new concept in business software: the fully-integrated, multitask, executive worksheet. This is a fancy name for one package that puts different programs together and lets you move data from one into another. Several of these are already on the market, and more are on the way. One of the first to hit the market was *Context MBA* (Context Management Systems). This revolutionary new program sells for $695 and integrates five applications, including business modeling, graph-making, word processing, telecommunications, and database functions. Another integrated package is called *1–2–3*. Available from Lotus Development Corporation for $495, it integrates modeling, graphics, and database management.

Context MBA obviously does more than *1–2–3*. On the other hand, it costs more and is more difficult to learn to use well. Which is better? Again, there is no simple answer. You'll have to decide for yourself. An article in the June 1983 issue of *INC. Magazine* might help you do that. It is an in-depth comparison of *MBA* and *1–2–3*, by Robert A. Mamis.

Also muddying the waters is a new product by VisiCorp called *Visi/ON*. *Visi/ON* takes the integrated worksheet concept one step farther. This software system is designed to integrate any number of programs so that data can be passed from one to the other. The software uses a *window* approach. You can open different windows on your display screen and view data from several programs at once. In addition, *Visi/ON* will allow you to move the cursor and select options with a hand-held piece of hardware called a *mouse*. (The function of a mouse is explained in Chapter Ten.) VisiCorp believes *Visi/ON* has the potential to become the standard software used to integrate various business programs. No price had been set for *Visi/ON* when this book was written.

All spreadsheets turn your computer into a giant worksheet, but there is real difference in size. The single-purpose worksheets, like *VisiCalc*, *SuperCalc*, and *Multiplan*, all have about 63 columns and 254 rows. *MBA* has 95 columns and 999 rows. *1–2–3* is the largest, with 256 columns and 2048 rows. If you are doing sophisticated financial planning, *1–2–3* has some obvious advantages. For one thing, you can put all the information on the spreadsheet at one time. Your balance sheet, income statement, and sales forecast are all there all of the time. But do you really need all this power? Again, that depends on your application. One published evaluation of the worksheets available is in Chapter Six of the book *All About 1–2–3* (dilithium Press). As you can imagine, the authors are somewhat prejudiced towards *1–2–3*, but they do analyze several different kinds of worksheets.

Business Planner

Business Planner works a lot like an electronic spreadsheet but is really a special-purpose software package intended to help managers and owners of small businesses evaluate their business and develop adequate plans for the future. It will accept a variety of data and help you develop business plans, charts, graphs, and figures. It will also generate models of your business that help you analyze the future outcomes of present practices, and it helps you ask and answer *What if* questions. It would take a whole chapter just to describe all the variables this program handles and its features. If you manage the operation of a small business, this $395 program is one you should consider.

Database Management

A database management program will help you keep track of the mountains of information needed to conduct business. They are really electronic filing systems. Why do you need an electronic filing system? One reason is that you probably have lots of wasteful duplication in the way you currently maintain your files. A personnel department, for example, probably has quite a bit of information on each employee. They have to keep track of data like names, addresses, next of kin, and so on. The sales department probably also maintains a file on each salesperson. These files contain some unique information but probably also much of the same information that is in the personnel files. Within departments, it's the same story. Duplication is wasteful of time and space, and that translates to dollars and cents.

If you are currently doing some of your business information housekeeping with computers, you probably still have the same problem. You may be using a payroll program and also a program to keep track of the amount and type of each sale made by each salesperson in your department. The ideal way to handle information for these purposes is to have one central electronic file which is accessed by all other programs. That eliminates duplication and saves money. It also means that you can centralize your *data gathering* efforts. Since there is only one file, you can be very thorough and do a really good job. When information needs to be updated, it only has to be entered once.

Small businesses are not the only ones that can use database management programs. If you keep any type of information in an organized system, a database management system may help you automate functions now done by hand. Any information that must be organized, categorized, and filed is a candidate for computerization. Here are some of the popular database management programs.

dBASE II

dBASE II is one of the Cadillacs of database management systems for the IBM PC. There's good news and bad news about this software. The good news is that the program is very flexible and can do a super job if you use it correctly. The bad news is that the program is expensive ($700) and difficult to learn to use well.

dBASE II is what is known as a *relational database* system. What that means, in a nutshell, is that the program makes it easy to pull out and understand the relationships among information bits stored in the system. For example, suppose you decide you want to know the relationship among total sales in February, number of salespeople on the road that month and the previous month, and the amount of money spent on advertising over the past six months. Using separate paper-and-pencil files, that information could be hard to get at. With *dBASE II*, it would be at your fingertips.

Reviewers of this program have said it has *almost unlimited flexibility*. You'll have to pay a price, of course, and the seven hundred dollars may be only the beginning. The real price is in terms of complexity. This program is not for beginners! Learning to use *dBASE II* has been compared to learning to speak a new language! You don't just slip the disk in and go with *dBASE II*. If you have no programming experience, you may want to consider a less powerful but easier-to-learn program.

But if you have a business operation with information problems, and if you or someone in your organization has had some experience with computers, *dBASE II* may be exactly what you need.

One piece of good news is that you can give the program a try without risking seven hundred dollars. When the program arrives, it comes with a sample disk to allow you to try out the program. If you aren't happy, don't unpack the real program. Just send it back for a full refund. That's a nice touch. You'll need at least 96K and one disk drive to run this program.

Data Base Manager

Data Base Manager (Alpha Software Corporation) is a database management system designed for people who don't have the expertise or the need for a system as complex and sophisticated as *dBASE II*. *Data Base Manager* sells for $185 and offers a surprising number of features for such an inexpensive package.

You can search for information a variety of ways, including by zip code or by date. There is a special search that uses phonetic clues to help find a name or address if you aren't sure of the correct spelling. The program will search for entries that sound similar when spoken orally. You can use *Data Base Manager* if you have at least 64K of memory and two disk drives.

This program is quick and easy to learn, and the manual has a good tutorial, including an instructional audio tape. This is an excellent compromise if you need a fast electronic file but you really don't need an expensive and complex system. *Data Base Manager* would be a good first database management system.

DataEase

DataEase is a general-purpose database management program from Software Solutions. It lists for $595 and runs on an IBM PC with 128K of RAM and two disk drives. This menu-driven program displays a list of options on the screen and lets you select what you want to do by entering the number beside the option you want.

This program, while expensive, has some very nice features. First, it is not as difficult to learn to use as several of the other powerful database management systems. Second, it takes advantage of the color features of the IBM PC in its displays, a feature not often found in business software.

PFS:File

PFS:File is one of a whole set of programs from PFS known for its ease of use. *PFS:File* may not be the most powerful of the database management programs, but it provides a nice combination of ease of use and power. It has one of the best written manuals in this category. The ad for *PFS:File* says it "is basically a paper filing system without the paper. So you can record, file, retrieve and review information in a fraction of the time it takes with a conventional filing system." We agree; it is a good program for $140. The version for the IBM is distributed by IBM.

Data Design

This program is another easy-to-use database management package, published by Insoft for $225. It also has an excellent manual with a nice introduction to the concept of database management software and their uses in American business. A useful feature of *Data Design* is a built-in telecommunications program that makes it easy to transfer data and files from one computer to the other over phone lines.

KnowledgeMan

KnowledgeMan is a $500 program from Micro Data Base Systems. This is not a program for the beginner. It may not even be a program for the intermediate user! This is a complex, integrated program that combines the features of an electronic spreadsheet, a database management program, and more. Although not as well-known as programs like *SuperCalc*, *dBASE II*, *1-2-3*, or *MBA*, *KnowledgeMan* has the features of those programs and some additional ones. You pay for those features in complexity. This is not a program you will be able to learn in a weekend. If you are serious about managerial applications of your computer, and you need a sophisticated program with many features, you may want to consider *KnowledgeMan*. The program comes with a thick manual; a book called *Using KnowledgeMan* should be published by Que Corporation by the time you read this. In addition, Micro Data Base Systems plans to offer training seminars in various parts of the country for *KnowledgeMan* users. They also plan to sell a beginner's tutorial manual and a video cassette on the program. You may need all the help you can get to learn this very complex but useful program.

Mini Data Base Manager

Mini Data Base Manager (Software Laboratories) is a good program for you if you are a little unsure about what a database management system can do. This little program can handle only three files of 100 records each. This's not big enough for many tasks, but it will give you a taste of what database management is all about. It has good sorting and editing capabilities, too. It only costs $10, and when you're through with it, you might be able to turn it over to your son or daughter. A child could use it to help manage a paper route or something like that.

Other Business Software for Your IBM PC

There are many other business uses for the IBM PC computer that we haven't talked about. For instance, you can do in-depth research on business topics using the Management Contents function on The Source. The Source is described in Chapter Six. With the space in this book we cannot even review briefly all the different business applications possible with the IBM PC and appropriate software. We will give you a brief description of some of the other programs.

TeloFacts

TeloFacts is a new kind of program available from dilithium Software. This software is *documentation*-based rather than *program*-based. The documentation for *TeloFacts* is a book,

How To Use TeloFacts, which is available separately for $9.95. The program helps you design and use questionnaires. The book not only teaches you how to use the program, it also teaches you how to design questionnaires.

The program can be used for any questionnaire with multiple-choice answers. The questionnaires don't even have to be questions; they could be categories on an application form. For instance, a personnel manager could use the program to evaluate job applicants. A bank loan officer could use it to evaluate loan applications, and a teacher could use it for testing. It is primarily used though for marketing surveys. It will rank, score, and evaluate the answers to any set of questions. *TeloFacts 1* sells for $49.95 and is available in many bookstores. *TeloFacts 2* is a more sophisticated version of the program that sells for $195. The strongest feature of this program is that it is extremely easy to use.

Mail-XI

This program combines mailing list and report writing capabilities. You can enter all the standard mailing information, such as name, address, city, and state. You also enter remarks when you need them. Searches can be conducted in a variety of ways.

The report writer can be used to print labels or lists of names and addresses after searches are carried out. *Mail-XI* (Micro Architect) sells for $288. Without the report writer it sells for $198.

Mailtrak

There are many mailing list programs available for the IBM PC. *Mailtrak* is a good, moderately priced program ($65) from TCI Software. It stores up to 1200 names, including two address lines, plus city, state, nine digit zip code, two phone numbers, five mail codes and four activity codes with dates. The program prints out telephone directories, master lists, mailing labels, and files that can be used in word processing programs such as *EasyWriter*.

EZLabel

EZLabel is a no-frills mailing list program that stores up to 1000 names and addresses. Searches may be conducted by zip code, last name, or by categories you have created. The program will also print mailing labels. You'll need 48K, one disk drive, and a printer. This program from Systemics sells for $39.95.

Dow Jones Stock Analyzer

This program helps the serious investor who uses the online database called the Dow Jones News/Retrieval Service and wants to store the data on disk, update it later, and chart it numerically and graphically. The *Dow Jones Analyzer* is available for approximately $350 from Dow Jones and Company, Inc./RTR Software.

Investors refer to this program as a tool for *technical analysis*. This is investor jargon for looking at how a stock has done in the past to try to figure out how it will do in the future.

The program is easy to use, and a sample lesson is included with the package. You are given multiple-choice menu options, and you press a key to tell the program what you want. If

Figure 8.6   SofTax

you're into technical analysis, you will be interested in the *Dow Jones Stock Analyzer*.

SofTax

This is another *VisiCalc* support program. It costs $395 and is available from Design Trends. The program lets you enter data related to your tax situation and will analyze your current and future tax liabilities, as well as help you prepare your tax reports. The program allows you to ask *What if* questions about taxes. For example, you can use the program to evaluate the effects of income averaging on your tax bill.

Invest

Invest, a $125 program from Miracle Computing, takes over the record keeping and accounting chores involved in managing a portfolio of securities.

The Apartment House Manager

This program from User-Friendly Software takes over some of the business and accounting tasks of managing an apartment complex. It includes five programs. You can store tenant information, print form letters to tenants, and take care of your accounting chores, including printing monthly profit-and-loss statements. This software requires 64K, one drive, and a printer. The program sells for $395.

IBM Business Series Program Packages

IBM sells many business programs for their computer. Their *Business Series Program Packages* include titles such as *Accounts Receivable*, *General Ledger*, *General Accounting*, and *Inventory Control*. They also sell a *Professional Series* including such programs as *Time Management* and *VisiCalc*.

CHAPTER NINE

Programming

As you read this book, or any other book on computers, you will read about computer programs. Even if you've never read about computers, you've probably heard the word *program* mentioned in relation to computers.

In this chapter you will learn what a computer program is and a little about how programs are made. You will not learn how to program, but rather what kind of programming can be done on the IBM PC and how programming fits into the total picture of what you can do with your computer. Also in this chapter, we will show you some examples of what the different languages look like. The sample programs are only intended to give you a picture of how the languages differ. If you want to learn programming, the place to start is with the instruction manual for your computer or with a good book on how to program in a particular language.

WHAT DOES PROGRAMMING HAVE TO DO WITH USING A COMPUTER?

Your IBM PC (and every other computer) can only do what it is told to do. The computer, with all its parts in order, is still just a tool waiting to be used. Not only does it have to be told what to do, but also how to do it. The process of telling the computer what to do is called programming. To put it more precisely: without a program, your computer is just a collection of parts.

WHO WRITES COMPUTER PROGRAMS?

Not so long ago, only a few highly skilled, specially trained people wrote programs to tell computers what to do. That has changed. Today millions of people know how to write programs and thousands more are learning every day. Even very young children can now program computers. No, this isn't because people have gotten smarter. It's because computers have become much easier to program.

There are different levels of programming. The people who did the built-in programming for your computer are highly skilled. They understand electronics and how computers work. Other programmers are less conversant with the inner workings of the computer but make their living writing programs that make computers do things people want them to do. These programs are called software. Thanks to the professional programmers, you don't have to write a program to tell your computer everything you want it to do. You use programs other people have written.

SHOULD YOU LEARN TO PROGRAM?

It is possible for you to enjoy your IBM PC and to have it do a lot of work for you without ever learning how to program. Most software you can buy will give you an easy-to-follow set of directions. Once you gain some familiarity with your computer, you may choose from a wide variety of software. However, many computer owners enjoy learning how to program. Learning to program has the following advantages:

• Added enjoyment.—It is fun to be able to give the computer your own instructions and have it understand and follow them.

• Special uses.—Sometimes there just won't be any software available that will let you do what you want with your computer. If you gain enough skills in programming, you can write your own programs to get the computer to do exactly what you want it to do.

• Understanding software.—A person who knows something about programming is sometimes in a better position to select and use appropriate software. This depends on how much the person knows about programming and the nature of the software.

• Modifying software.—Sometimes a piece of software will do almost what you want, but not quite. If you know enough about programming, you may be able to modify the software to get it to do what you want.

COMPUTER LANGUAGES

The IBM PC in your home or business understands several computer languages. No, it doesn't converse fluently in French or Spanish, but it does understand a language called BASIC, as well as Logo, FORTRAN, and Pascal. The concept of a *computer language* is difficult for new computer owners. What is a computer language, and what role does it play in the computer?

The first thing you should know is that computer languages serve much the same purpose as human languages. They are a means of communication. Consider the way two people communicate. Assume you are a cooking instructor. Today you are going to teach a student how to cook a souffle. Because you and the student both speak English, you can give your instructions in English. This means English is your language or medium of communication. The information you communicate to the student in English is a specific, step-by-step set of instructions. *Recipe* is the special term used to describe such a set of directions when you are cooking.

If your student speaks French, and you speak only English, you may have a very strange looking souffle! To get what you want, you must have a common language. The same thing can happen with a computer. Computers like the IBM PC speak their own set of languages. Computers cannot learn English, so you will need to learn one of the languages the computer understands. When you learn a computer language like BASIC, you can communicate with the computer much as a master cook communicates with a student. Instead of communicating recipes, you will give the computer *programs*. A computer program is an organized set of instructions that tell the computer how to accomplish a particular goal. All the software reviewed in this book are really programs someone has written to tell the computer how to do a job. Programs, like recipes, are created by humans.

Learning to program a computer is not something everyone should do. Learning how to use the computer to do a job or play a game is just as honorable as becoming an experienced computer programmer. Learn to program the computer only if you find programming interesting.

LEVELS OF COMPUTER LANGUAGE

Suppose you are thinking of learning a second human language. If your first language is English, there are some languages, like French and Spanish, that are similar to yours. Others, like Greek and Latin, are not as similar, but contain some familiar elements. Still other languages, like Japanese and Chinese, are so different that few elements will be familiar to you. To learn Chinese, you need to learn a completely new alphabet that bears no resemblance to the one you learned as a child. In addition, the way information is organized is quite different.

If you decide to learn a computer language, you will find

the analogy relates. Some, like BASIC, are not exactly English but have enough similarities so you don't feel completely abandoned by your native tongue. Others, like FORTRAN or Pascal, are not so much like English but contain some familiar phrases or terms. Still others, like 8086 machine or assembly language bear little resemblance, if any, to English. We would advise you to learn one of the more English-like languages before tackling an assembly or machine language.

Computer languages have two basic parts: the vocabulary and the rules for using the vocabulary. These rules are usually referred to as the grammar. The word PRINT, for example, is a part of the vocabulary used in the IBM PC's BASIC. When the computer finds this word in a program it looks for material to display on the screen. A rather extensive set of rules tells you how to organize and punctuate the material after PRINT. These instructions tell the computer exactly how you want your material displayed on the screen. It is relatively easy to remember that PRINT is one of the words in the vocabulary of BASIC and to remember what PRINT tells the computer to do. Things are not so easy with some languages.

HIGH-LEVEL LANGUAGES

BASIC is only one of several languages that make up the category of *high-level languages*. High-level computer languages use English-like words and work with decimal numbers (the type we learned to add, subtract, multiply, and divide in grade school). While the other two families of languages, machine and assembly languages, are written specifically for a particular *computer*, high-level languages are often developed for a particular *purpose*. One of the older computer languages, FORTRAN (FORmula TRANslator), for example, is the language most used by universities and scientists. COBOL (COmmon Business Oriented Language) is a popular business language, and BASIC (Beginners All Purpose Symbolic Instruction Code) is the best known of the easy-to-learn general-purpose computer languages. Every popular personal computer sold today understands at least one, if not several, dialects of BASIC.

Several different programming languages are available for the IBM PC. While there are over 150 different languages, computers understand only one. Does this sound confusing? We will explain.

PROGRAMMING LANGUAGES FOR THE IBM PC

BASIC for the IBM PC

The obvious place to begin is with the language that comes with the IBM PC—BASIC. BASIC is the most popular programming language in use today, especially with small computers like the IBM PC. It is a high-level general purpose language that can be used for almost any type of programming and is many times easier to learn and to use than low-level languages like machine or assembly language. If you want the computer to put a certain word on the computer screen you can tell it to PRINT that word. Or if you want the computer to add 3 and 2 and assign the sum to the variable named X, you can just tell it to "LET $X = 3 + 2$".

If dealing with so many different computer languages is not confusing enough, there is one more complication. Not only are there over 150 different languages, there are also many different versions of each language. Just as there are many different dialects of French or English, there are also many different dialects of BASIC. In part that's because we need different tools to do different jobs. You probably always use a hammer to pound a nail, but you may use a roofing hammer to pound roofing nails and another hammer when you put a desk together for your den.

Another reason for the many different dialects of BASIC is that different computer manufacturers keep refining a language to keep pace with the new hardware and software they develop. The IBM PC, like most personal computers, has more than one dialect of BASIC. When you turn on the power to the IBM PC and wait for just a moment, you can program in a version of BASIC called BASIC 1.1. When you use the disk drive system, you have access to a more advanced dialect of BASIC called BASICA. With the addition of the IBM XT to the IBM Personal Computer family, there's a new version of BASIC called BASIC 2.0.

The differences among these three dialects are more technical than practical, especially if you are a beginning programmer. BASIC 1.1, the built-in version, is a good but limited version of BASIC. BASICA is a more advanced version and requires one or more floppy disk drives. Consequently, about the only time you ever use BASIC 1.1 is if you are working on a computer without disk drives. BASIC 2.0 lets you use the hard disk drive built into the IBM PC-XT.

Other dialects of BASIC that run on the IBM PC are sold by third-party software companies. Some of the third-party BASIC's are *compiled* so they run faster. A compiler program translates the instructions of a program written in BASIC back into machine language all at one time. The program, now in machine language, is then stored in memory or on disk. Now when you run the program, it runs very fast. BASIC 1.1, BASICA, and BASIC 2.0, on the other hand, are interpreter programs. An *interpreter program* translates the BASIC instructions to machine language as the program is running. The program is always stored in BASIC. Interpreted languages are easier to learn and use than compiled languages, but are much slower.

At most IBM dealers, you can buy a version of BASIC called BASIC Compiler. This product is sold by SuperSoft and sells for $300. Another compiler with many good features has gained popularity among IBM PC programmers: Microsoft's BASIC Compiler, which is available from IBM. It also sells for $300. The Microsoft program translates interpreter programs into compiled programs. These give you the best of both worlds. You get the programming ease of an interpreter program and the speed of a compiled program.

Pascal

Pascal is another high-level general-purpose language that runs on the IBM PC. If you are interested in programming in Pascal, PASCAL/M is available from Sorcim Corporation for $700. It will satisfy most of your needs and is easy to use. Another popular version is UCSD p-System PASCAL from IBM Corporation Systems Products Division. The UCSD part of the name means it is a dialect of Pascal developed at the University of California at San Diego. It sells for $625. The real advantage to the UCSD system is that it is now available for most small computers. Therefore, if you invest the time in learning this version of Pascal, you could use your programming skills on different brands of computers.

PILOT

PILOT is short for Programming Inquiry Learning Or Teaching. This is another specialized high-level language and, as the name suggests, it was designed to be used in education. There is an IBM-compatible version of PILOT called PILOT Language available from Laboratory Microsystems for $200. You will need the CP/M86 operating system to use this program.

Logo

Logo is a specialized high-level language designed to help children learn and to help them learn about computers. It is a very interesting and easy-to-use language. A more detailed discussion of Logo is presented in Chapter Four.

Two versions of Logo are available for the IBM PC. One is called MIT Logo and is sold by Krell Software Corporation. This version requires only the regular disk operating system (MS-DOS) that comes with your disk drives for the IBM PC.

This version is too expensive for our tastes, however. It sells for $2000.

A second version of Logo for the IBM PC is DR LOGO. It costs much less than the Krell version, with prices ranging from $150 to $200. DR LOGO was developed by Digital Research. DR LOGO seems to be the most serious attempt yet to develop a dialect of Logo that takes advantage of the strengths of the IBM PC.

Low-Level Languages: Machine and Assembly

The computer actually understands only one language—machine language. But machine language is not a single language. Each computer chip has its own set of instructions built by the designers. Instructions given the computer in any other language than its own machine language must first be translated into the machine language used by its CPU before it can understand and process the instructions. The IBM PC can understand BASIC only because IBM put BASIC in the computer's memory. When you use BASICA, the instructions that let the computer speak that language are loaded into RAM from a disk.

The IBM PC uses the 8088 microprocessor chip and can thus be programmed in 8088 machine language. One of the most trying things about machine language programming is that the symbols used for the instructions are numbers, and not even decimal numbers at that. They give you no indication of their meaning. Unless you memorize the numbers and their meaning, programming in machine language can be a boring, slow-paced procedure punctuated by searches through the table of instruction codes. We recommend you put off learning machine language until you are comfortable with one or two high-level languages.

In between BASIC and machine language is something called *assembly language*. Assembly languages let you use letters instead of numbers to give the computer instructions. For example, the number 06 might tell the computer to Load something into the CPU in machine language, while the letters LD might accomplish the same thing in assembly language. That makes it easier to write programs in assembly language, but it is still much more difficult than writing programs in BASIC or some other high-level language. The advantages of programs written in machine or assembly language are that they operate much faster than programs in BASIC, and once they are written, the program does not require as much memory as a BASIC program that does the same thing. When speed of operation is important (for instance, in a video game that uses animated color graphics), the program will probably be written in something other than a high-level language. If you need speed or economic use of memory, machine or assembly language may be your cup of tea.

Your IBM PC is not ready to be programmed in assembly language when you turn it on. You will need to buy a software package called an *editor assembler*. The editor element in the package lets you write and revise programs. The assembler element changes your instructions written in assembly language to machine language so that the computer can act on them. Often these editor assembler packages have other special programs as well. Some of the most common special programs contained in editor/assembler packages are short programs already written in assembly language that you can easily include in any assembly language program you are writing. These short programs are called *subroutines* and are written to do things that many programmers will want the computer to do. A subroutine that will alphabetize a set of words, for example, is used in many programs. You can simply add it whenever you want to, and you wouldn't have to write that part of the program yourself.

As with everything else relating to the IBM PC, there are several different editor/assembler packages available. IBM sells the ASM86 Assembler, a complete editor assembler package for the PC.

Assembly language programming is not a good place to start learning to program. It is very difficult and there is a high risk you may become discouraged before you ever get the computer to do much. Start with BASIC, Logo, or some other high-level language.

SAMPLE PROGRAMS
IN SEVERAL LANGUAGES

To give you an idea of what the different languages look like, we will show you how a simple computer program looks in several languages. Keep in mind that there are many different dialects of each language; these programs are only intended to show you what a language looks like. You may not be able to type the program into your computer and get it to run. If you want to get started programming, you will need an instruction manual for the version of the language you are using with the IBM PC.

Each of the sample programs instruct the computer to do the same thing. The computer puts on the screen:

HI, I AM THE IBM PC
WHAT'S YOUR NAME?
You type your name, let's say Thomas Watson.
The computer puts on the screen:
NICE TO MEET YOU, THOMAS WATSON.

High-Level General-Purpose Programming

Let's start with BASIC. Two aspects of BASIC have made it so popular. First, it is a general-purpose language and can be used efficiently for almost any programming job. Second, it is easy to learn. If you have never learned a programming language and want to get started programming your IBM PC yourself, BASIC is a good place to start. The advantages of BASIC as your first language are:

• Every other brand of home computer can be programmed in BASIC. Even though the dialects are slightly different, you can easily adjust your programming skills to another computer.

• Since more programs are written in BASIC than any other language, you can adopt and adapt more programs for your own use than you could if the only language you knew was one other than BASIC.

• Since it is the easiest general-purpose language to learn, you can probably do more with less learning time and effort than with any other language.

Here's what our computer program could look like in BASIC:

```
10 PRINT "HI, I'M YOUR IBM PC"
20 INPUT "WHAT'S YOUR NAME"; N$
30 PRINT
40 PRINT "NICE TO MEET YOU,"; N$
50 END
```

Pascal, while it is much easier to use than assembly language, is more complicated than other high-level languages. Pascal has three main advantages:

• It is faster than other high-level languages.

• Because of the way Pascal is structured, a program written in this language is easy for another programmer to understand and modify.

• Because of its speed and power, Pascal is a more efficient language for some complex business and scientific uses.

Our sample program written in Pascal would look like this:

```
BEGIN
WRITE(OUTPUT, 'HI, I AM THE IBM PC');
WRITE(OUTPUT, 'COMPUTER. ');
WRITE(OUTPUT, 'WHAT IS YOUR NAME?');
READLN(INPUT, NAME);
WRITE(OUTPUT, 'NICE TO MEET YOU, ');
WRITE(OUTPUT, 'NAME');
END
```

Specialized Programming
for Teaching and Learning

Although enthusiasts of this group of languages claim they are really suited for many general purpose programming tasks, they are becoming popular primarily because they are effective for classroom uses and are easy and quick to learn. One such language is Logo. Chapter Four talks about Logo as an educational tool, so we need not say much more about it here. Remember that this language is so easy to get started with that young children can begin programming the computer after only a few minutes of instruction. If you have children who use your IBM PC, Logo would be a good investment. Our same simple little program could look like this in Logo:

```
TO GREET
CLEARSCREEN
PRINT (HI, I AM THE IBM PC)
PRINT (HOME COMPUTER)
PRINT (WHAT IS YOUR NAME?)
CALL READLINE "N
PRINT "HELLO,
PRINT :N
END
```

Another educationally oriented language is PILOT. PILOT is a language created for a specific purpose: to help teachers write teaching programs. These programs are called *computer-assisted instruction*. Many teachers do not have the kind of technical background required to quickly learn and use complex programming languages. Yet they are in a better position than anyone else to know what kinds of programs are most needed in their classrooms. PILOT is a language that teachers can learn quickly. It is designed to do the kind of programming required to get the computer to act as a teaching machine. PILOT is sometimes called a conversational language. With only a few programming skills, a teacher can write a program that seems to be able to carry on an informative conversation with the student.

PILOT is *not* the best general purpose language around. But, if you are a teacher or if you want to write educational programs for your children, you may want to get started with PILOT. PILOT is also a quick way to get children started programming. In PILOT our little illustration program might look like this:

```
D: R$(15)
T: HI, I AM THE IBM PC
T: COMPUTER
T: WHAT IS YOUR NAME?
A: R$
T: HI THERE $R$
E:
```

Low-Level Programming

With editor/assembler package, you can program your computer in assembly language. Remember that in this language you are only one step removed from the language the computer really understands, machine language. When you tell the computer to carry out the instructions you have given it in assembly language, a built-in program called an assembler translates your instructions into machine language, and the computer carries them out.

Although programming in assembly language is complicated and tedious, it has several advantages if you want to spend the time it takes to become familiar with it. Probably the greatest advantage is speed. Although your computer can do things quickly compared to how fast you can do them, sometimes a little additional speed is needed. Programs written in assembly language can do things much faster than programs written in high-level languages like BASIC.

A second advantage is that you can get the computer to do some things you can't get it to do in other languages. In this language you have total control over the computer; the only limits are those set by the engineering of the computer. In high-level languages, you are confined not only to the engineering limits of the machine, but also to limits of the language. Because assembly language gives you total control over the computer, you can use it in two different ways. First, when you need a program that is impossible or awkward to write in a high-level language, you can write the program in assembly language using an editor/assembler package. Second, instead of writing a whole program in assembly language, you can write a short program that does one special thing and then incorporate it into a BASIC or other high-level language program. Now let's see what this program might look like if you were-to write it in an assembly language:

```
              REF        WMBW,INPUT
LINE1         TEXT       'HI, I AM THE IBM PC'
LINE2         TEXT       'COMPUTER'
LINE3         TEXT       'WHAT'S YOUR NAME?'
BUFFER        BSS        32
LINE4         TEXT       'NICE TO MEET YOU,'
GREET         LI         R0,0
              LI         R1,LINE1
              LI         R2,32
              BLWP       @VMBW
              LI         R0,64
              LI         R1,LINE2
              BLWP       @VMBW
              LI         R0,128
              LI         R1,LINE3
              BLWP       @VMBW
              LI         R0,BUFFER
              BLWP       @INPUT
              LI         R0,256
              LI         R1,LINE4
              BLWP       @VMBW
              LI         R0,288
              LI         R1,BUFFER
              BLWP       @VMBW
              END        GREET
```

You can probabably see why we think you should learn another language first.

Even More Languages

There are many other languages available for the IBM PC that we haven't mentioned. Two of these are popular with large computers but not widely used with personal computers: FOR-TRAN and COBOL. These languages have been in use for a long time and have some special applications. If you have just purchased an IBM PC or are thinking about purchasing one and have done no programming, you will probably want to start with BASIC. But if you have used a language like COBOL or FORTRAN on a larger computer and feel comfortable with it, you will be glad to know you can talk to your new friend, the IBM PC, in a familiar language.

FORTRAN is a popular language with people who work with mathematical formulas. In fact, the name FORTRAN comes from the words *formula translation*. The IBM version of FORTRAN, IBM FORTRAN, costs $350. COBOL is another popular language on large computers. As the name suggests, it is a specialized language for business uses. COBOL uses many regular English words to give the computer directions. Although its use with personal computers is limited, it can be run on many brands and is available for the IBM PC. A compiled version of COBOL is sold by many IBM dealers for $700.

Some Special Tools for Programming

In addition to the various computer languages, many other programming tools are available to help you write programs. These are designed either to give you shortcuts in programming or to speed up the running of your program once you have written it.

For example, Advanced Operating Systems sells a product

called *The Program Bit*. This program helps you organize and design a program. You can even take some shortcuts in the actual programming process. By shortcuts we mean that you will be able to use one instruction to accomplish what would otherwise take a series of instructions to accomplish. This program has more use for the professional programmer than for someone just getting started. Programs like *The Program Bit* are difficult to understand if you are not already experienced in BASIC or some other language. If you are an experienced programmer and are looking for some specialized tools to add to your programming tool kit, *The Program Bit* could be of value to you. It sells for $1,500.

Another useful program is *VEDIT*, a program distributed by CompuView Products. *VEDIT* is short for Visual Editor. The program, which works much like a standard word processing program, has features that make it easy to write, edit, and revise programs.

VEDIT performs a relatively routine but useful function in the process of writing programs. That is not the case with *Next Step*, a program from Execuware, a division of Aeronca, which is better known as one of the old-line manufacturers of single engine airplanes. *Next Step* is for people who don't want to learn to program in a language like BASIC but need special software for their computer that is not available commercially. *Next Step* can best be described as a program generator. It has the characteristics of database management programs described in the business chapter, but it does even more. You can customize the way data are manipulated and displayed. If you use your computer for business applications and need to store and manipulate data in ways not accommodated in standard programs, you may want to check out *Next Step*.

As you have seen, there are many different languages available for the IBM PC. Initially you will probably be content with the BASIC that comes with the computer. At some point, though, you may want to expand your programming tool kit to include other dialects of BASIC or other languages. The decision is always complicated, but is even more complicated with the IBM PC because there are so many alternatives. We strongly suggest that when you consider using any language other than BASICA, you explore your options carefully. Make sure you clearly understand what you need to use that language on your computer. It is very easy to get caught in the trap of always needing just one more piece of hardware or software to be able to use the language of your choice.

CHAPTER TEN

Peripherals

This chapter might have been subtitled: *Ways to Spend Your Money*. Peripherals, or accessories, are the extra pieces of hardware you buy for your computer to get it to do different jobs. Buying peripherals for your computer is a little like shopping for options for a new car. Each option for the car makes it a little nicer, and each one has a price tag. The same thing is true of computer peripherals. There is a difference, however. Peripherals for your IBM PC can easily cost several times the cost of the basic computer!

WHERE TO BUY ACCESSORIES

Where should a new IBM PC owner buy accessories? If you subscribe to magazines like *PC* and *PC World*, you will see ads from many mail-order companies with toll-free numbers. Call them up, give your VISA or MASTERCARD number, and they ship products to you by return mail. Prices for products through the mail are often ten to thirty-five percent lower than the price of comparable products in local stores. Should you buy locally or through the mail?

We buy about half our computer accessories and software through the mail and half from local stores. In our opinion, beginners should seriously consider buying mostly from local stores. For one thing, a good store will have someone who can give advice, suggestions, and hints, as well as take your money.

But a good store can be hard to find. In some, the only thing the salesperson can do is point you in the direction of the counter with IBM PC accessories and ask if that will be cash or credit card. Even with that type of store, it is usually easier to get an adjustment when a problem occurs. If the product doesn't work or the software doesn't load, the store will usually exchange it or refund the purchase price. A mail-order company will usually do the same thing, but you must return the product first. It can take several weeks to straighten out a problem, even if the mail-order supplier is cooperative.

There is one area where mail-order suppliers generally have an advantage. Few local stores carry the variety of products available by mail. Several mail-order companies carry several hundred products for the IBM PC; few retail stores can match that. Sometimes the only source for a product you want will be a mail-order supplier.

Whether you buy locally or by mail-order, there are some hazards you should be aware of. Local stores often have salespeople who don't understand your computer. Instead of telling you they don't know the answer to a question, they'll give you the answer they think is most likely to make a sale. If we go into a store where we're not sure of the salespeople, we ask a few questions we know the answers to. If the salesperson answers them accurately and honestly, even if the answers reduce the likelihood of a sale, we can put more confidence in the answers that person gives to other questions. This technique has produced some astounding answers.

The people who answer the phone at a mail-order supplier can also provide inaccurate information. Perhaps the best advice is to be very careful about making buying decisions on the basis of what a salesperson, especially one working on a commission, tells you. This may be doing a disservice to many fine salespeople, but they are a minority in this field. We feel a store that has a good sales staff is worth an extra ten to fifteen percent, because their knowledge and advice can save you much more than that.

A common problem with mail-order companies is delays in shipping products. Think twice about ordering something that is not in stock. Many companies will tell you they are expecting a big shipment *on Friday* and will be glad to ship yours that afternoon. Big shipments are often late in this industry because companies cannot keep up with demand. That Friday shipment may not get there for five or six Fridays. And even if the shipment does arrive, there may be so many back orders that your order cannot be filled. It is not uncommon for mail-order suppliers to charge the cost of a product to your credit card the day you place the order and then take weeks, even months, to send that product to you. Of course, there are honest, responsible mail-order suppliers who do everything they can to provide quick service. As with local suppliers, we feel that type of company is worth a little extra cost because it saves you lots of frustration.

Extra Memory

The older IBM PC came with 16K of memory on the main computer board. You could expand the memory to 64K by plugging memory chips into sockets already installed on the board. After the first 64K you could not simply plug in additional chips. Adding more memory required you to plug in special memory cards. These cards plug into one of the standard expansion slots inside the computer.

The new versions of the IBM PC let you add up to 256K of memory by plugging in chips. After 256K you must again revert to adding memory on memory cards.

The easiest method of adding memory is to take your IBM PC down to the store where you bought it and pay them to add extra memory. That is also the most expensive approach. When this section of the book was written, an extra 64K of memory at a local IBM PC dealer cost $150. We were able to buy the chips needed to add 64K ourselves for $40 at a local discount supplier. Those chips took about ten minutes to install in the sockets already on the circuit board, and they worked fine.

If you want to expand the memory of your computer beyond the maximum possible by simply plugging in chips, you have several options:

• You can buy a memory board made by IBM and plug it in. That is the most expensive way to add memory cards.

• You can buy a memory board made by someone other than IBM and plug it in. These memory boards generally save you from one-third to one-half the cost of a comparable IBM board. At least fifty different companies manufacture memory boards for the IBM PC at this point. You can buy regular boards, for example, that add 128K of memory and are not expandable. Or you can buy a board with 128K of chips installed but which also has blank sockets where additional memory can be added later. We think buying an expandable memory board is the best option. If you only want to add 128K, buy a board with that much memory installed, but get one that lets you add more memory later should you need it (everybody needs more memory, sooner or later).

Memory boards from reputable third-party manufacturers like TecMar and QuadRam are, we feel, as good as those made by IBM. They just cost less. One problem you should be aware of is the possibility that a board is incompatible with your version of the IBM PC. If you have one of the early machines that could handle no more than 64K on the main board, some memory cards designed for the new version will not work. And memory boards designed for the older version of the PC may not work with new models that let you add 256K right on the board. Before buying a board, be sure it is compatible with your version of the PC.

• A final option for memory is to buy a combination card that gives you extra memory and several other features on the same plug-in card. We will discuss some of those cards later.

If you're squeamish about what you add to your IBM PC, the best approach is probably to add only IBM-produced products. That will put you at ease, and it will certainly make IBM happy. If, on the other hand, you are the least bit adventuresome, you may want to consider buying accessories and cards made by third-party suppliers. In many instances these cards combine on one card the functions of several cards made by IBM. Since the PC has a limited number of expansion slots, the advantage of combination cards is that they leave slots free for other functions. Most combination cards are made by third-party suppliers.

Video Game Controllers

One of those extra slots could be used for a game control adapter. If you add the game control adapter, you can plug in a variety of game controllers, including joysticks and game paddles.

Educational and recreational uses of the IBM PC often call for a means of input other than the keyboard. Many arcade games do not work well if you must press keys to control movement. A wide variety of video game controllers are available today that can be used on the IBM PC. We used a *Pointmaster* joystick from Discwasher, which is more expensive than many joysticks but got better ratings from confirmed game players.

If you are shopping for joysticks, you may want to test-drive several before buying. Joysticks vary considerably in their feel and fit, and if they don't fit your playing style, they can cause fatigue and low scores. Some people feel that the inexpensive joystick made by ATARI is difficult to use because you can't feel when you've moved the stick far enough to register. Others find its post too small and too short.

Companies such as Discwasher, Spectravision, Suncom, and Wico manufacture higher priced but more adaptable models in a variety of formats and styles. Wico's *Famous Red Ball* joystick, for example, costs $35, is sturdily built, and has two strategically placed fire buttons. Wico, which also manufactures joysticks and trackballs for arcade games, has a large line of products, including the *Power Grip* joystick ($37), which has a large handle that fits your hand, and a deluxe model ($45) that comes with three different interchangeable handles.

There are more versions of the traditional joystick than any other type, but at least a few models of several other game controllers are also available for the IBM PC. Both Wico and

TG Products sell a *trackball* game controller that can be substituted for a joystick. Trackballs let you roll a large round ball set in the top of a controller to direct the action of a game. They are quicker and more precise than many joysticks (for some games), but are generally much more expensive.

You can also buy radically different joysticks, like Zircon's *Video Command*, a cigar-shaped device with a triangular controller on top that can be moved by your thumb, and *Le Stick*, another fat cigar-style joystick that you control by tilting your hand in the direction you want it to go. One of our favorite controllers for the IBM PC is the Wico *Command*, another cigar-shaped joystick with a triangular post at the top.

Keyboard Enhancements

We discussed the problems of the keyboard that comes with the IBM PC in Chapter One and described some of the enhancements available for it. We will only repeat here the comment that several companies, including Keytronics, sell a

Figure 10.1   Trackball

keyboard that replaces the IBM PC keyboard. We don't like the keyboard on the PC and will spend the $200 to replace it with a Keytronic unit. Friends who own PCs argue that the standard keyboard is just fine. They say they adjusted to it after only a few hours of work with the computer. If you don't make the adjustment, keep the availability of replacement keyboards in mind.

Video Enhancement Hardware

We have already discussed the video format used by the IBM PC, including its use of two somewhat incompatible video display cards, the monochrome card and the color/graphics card. Several non-IBM video display products are available for the IBM PC. We'll describe some of the more popular ones.

USI Multidisplay Card. This circuit card plugs into one of the expansion slots and gives you something you cannot get from any card produced by IBM. You can use either the monochrome video display format or the color/graphics format with this one board. You can even use two monitors at once. The card includes the two video interfaces, plus a parallel printer interface and memory used to store high-resolution graphics data. The card comes from USI Computer Products and costs $495.

Amdek Multiple Adaptor Interface Board. Amdek is a major supplier of computer peripherals and seems to have a hit with this card. On one board you get 128K of memory expansion, a connection for a light pen, a parallel printer interface, and the circuits needed to use either the monochrome display format or the color/graphics format. It also has a feature that lets you customize the characters displayed by the PC. The price is $599.

Hercules Graphics Card. This $499 card lets you use the features of the color/graphics card from IBM, but it connects to an ordinary monochrome monitor instead of a color monitor. This popular video card for the PC is available from Hercules Computer Technology. Keep in mind that although it does not give you color output, it lets you use the high-resolution graphics of a color system on a regular monochrome monitor.

ColorPlus Graphics Board. This $475 board is available from Plantronics/Frederick Electronics Corporation. The board comes with a software package called the *Draftsman* that lets you create high-quality color graphics on the PC. Like some of the graphics software reviewed in Chapter Three, this program can send graphics to a color monitor, a dot matrix printer, or a printer/plotter (Hewlett-Packard). Your graphic creations can also be stored on a disk and then displayed as if they were video slides on the color monitor. The graphics produced by this product are outstanding.

Orchid Graphics Adapter. This product is produced by Orchid Technology. It costs $495 with software. Like the Hercules board, this one lets you use high-resolution graphics on an ordinary monochrome monitor. The *Orchid* board comes with software that gives you several additional keywords for creating graphics. You can use these keywords in BASICA along with the graphics keywords built into that language, or you can write programs that create graphics in other languages. *Orchid* also lets you send graphics to a dot matrix printer like the Epson FX-80.

Printers

Most printers aren't specially designed for a particular brand of computer. Therefore, many companies make printers for personal computers. At least a hundred different models will work with your IBM PC. To review them all would take far more space than we have in this chapter. Instead we will offer some general advice about printer shopping. Several of the magazines described at the end of Chapter One regularly publish articles on selecting printers for your computer. The book *Computers for Everybody* by Jerry Willis and Merl Miller (dilithium Press) also has a section on printer selection. You may want to consult these sources if you are shopping for a printer.

There are many things you need to think about before you

buy a printer: how fast can it print, what does the print look like, and does it have special functions? With printers, you are always dealing with trade-offs. If you choose a cheap one, you might find that the quality of the print is not what you want. Or you may find that it prints slowly and has no special features, such as the ability to print graphics. Although there are printers that cost less than $100 today, a good one can cost much more than the computer.

The printer situation today is far from gloomy, however. Things are getting better all the time. Some of the low-cost printers ($300 to $600) have good quality and reasonable speed along with some good special features.

There are two main types of printers for personal computers today: *dot matrix* and *daisy wheel*.

Dot Matrix Printers

These printers produce the type of print you can recognize as being printed by a computer. Each letter is formed by a series of dots. The quality of the print varies but is getting better all the time. Some of the newest models have such a tight pattern of dots that the letters look almost as if they were printed on a typewriter. Dot matrix printers are relatively cheap and fast. The major disadvantage is the quality of print. Since the print does not look exactly like typewriter print, they have not been considered *letter quality*. As the print quality gets better some people are beginning to use them for letter quality work.

If you primarily use a printer for printing out computer programs and graphics, this type of printer will work well for you. However, if your primary need is for word processing, you may want to look at another type.

You can select dot matrix printers from a staggering array of prices, qualities, and brands. Almost any computer store will have several models, ranging in price from a low of $300 to a high of $2000. These printers vary as much in speed and quality of print as they do in price. Our suggestion is that you go into your local computer store and ask for a demonstration.

One popular model is the Epson FX-80, which has a suggested retail price of $699. It is often sold for much less, however. It prints about three pages per minute and has some good special features, including the ability to print graphics. The printer sold by IBM for the PC is actually an older model of an Epson printer. Other manufacturers, like Okidata, Toshiba, IDS, C-Itoh, and Centronics, also make good quality dot matrix printers. Mannesman-Talley recently attracted attention with a fast dot matrix printer with high quality output that sells for less than $800.

Daisy Wheel Printers

This type of printer will print fully formed letters and characters as clear and crisp as those made by a typewriter. The letters are made up of solid images rather than dots. The daisy wheel printer gets its name from the print element. It looks like a daisy with long prongs coming out from a central wheel. There is a letter, number, or character at the end of each prong. The daisy wheel spins around at high speed. When the correct letter is in the correct location, a small hammer knocks it into the ribbon and leaves an imprint on the paper.

Until recently, these printers were expensive. Now they have begun to drop in price and are becoming competitive with dot matrix printers. The low cost daisy wheel printers, including the one from IBM, are very slow, however. The Smith Corona TP-1 prints 12.5 characters a second and costs around $550. At that speed, it would take the TP-1 20 minutes to print a ten page report. A dot matrix printer in that price range might print 80 to 100 characters a second.

Most printers use either a *serial* or a *parallel* interface. You don't get a standard serial or parallel interface in the lower-priced IBM PC models, which means adding a printer. Even the one from IBM will require you to add either a serial or parallel interface. Several companies, including IBM, sell these interfaces, and many of the combination boards include one or both types.

Light Pens

A light pen is a pen-like pointer connected to the computer. When you touch the light pen to the computer screen, the computer can determine the location of the pen on the screen. Light pens are used in a variety of ways. One common use is to indicate your choice on a multiple choice test or questionnaire. With the right software, you can use the light pen to draw pictures on the screen. You touch the pen to the screen and then, as you move it over the surface of the screen, it leaves a line just as if it were writing on the screen.

To use a light pen to draw graphics or select answers to a question on the screen you must have a program that tells the computer how to do it. One light pen system, which comes with software for the IBM PC, is produced by Symtec. This pen requires the color/graphics adapter card and sells for $150.

The Mouse

The mouse we are referring to is a computer mouse, a palm-size device with small wheels or a ball on the bottom. As the mouse is moved on a surface, the wheels or ball moves, and this movement is electronically coded and sent to the computer.

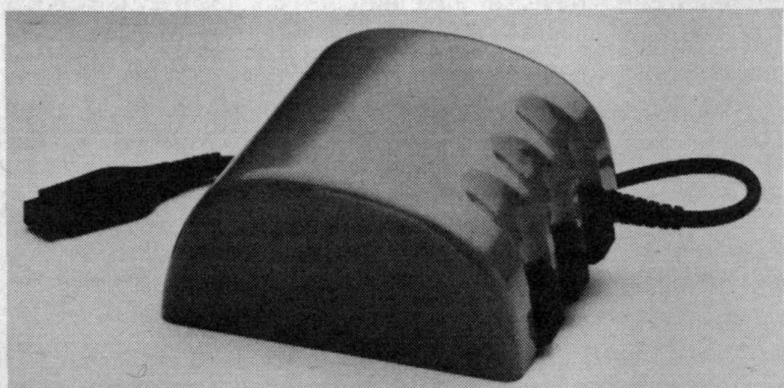

Figure 10.2   Mouse

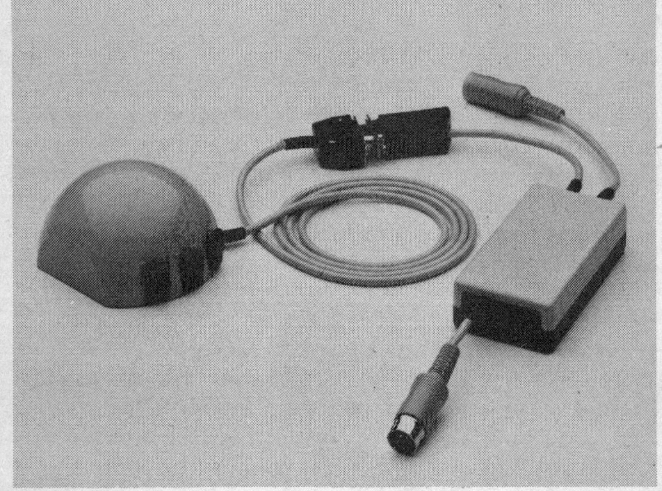

Figure 10.3   LogiMouse

The code received by the computer is generally used to move the cursor around on the screen. If you roll the mouse to the left on the desk the cursor on the screen moves to the left, for example.

Computer mice are just beginning to be used, but many magazines have high praise for computers and programs that use them. A program might present a menu on the screen and let you roll the mouse around until the cursor is over the option you want to select. Then you press a button on the mouse, and the computer knows what you want to do.

Another way to use the mouse is to move it around to create graphics on the screen. Perhaps we're old fashioned, but we aren't that impressed with mouse technology at this point. Thus far, we would just as soon press the A key on the computer keyboard to select option A on the screen rather than moving the mouse around. Our desks are usually so messy that the mouse would get lost anyway.

Some new generation computer software such as *Visi/ON* may use the mouse technology in much more sophisticated ways, however. Mouse devices are becoming popular; at least a dozen are available for the IBM PC. Mouse House is one of the leading manufacturers of these little critters. Their mechanical mouse sells for about $300, and you will need an interface, as well. Microsoft also makes a mouse that can be used with the IBM PC; their version sells for $195.

One interesting version of the electronic mouse is the *LogiMouse* produced by LogiTech for $375. The *LogiMouse* is made in Switzerland, and the adapter that lets you connect it to the IBM PC is made in Italy. The interface system, *LogiMate*, comes with three types of software. One type lets you use the mouse to move the cursor. (Any program that accepts cursor control signals from the keyboard will accept them from the *LogiMouse*.) The other two types let you use the mouse to generate signals the PC interprets as instructions to create various types of graphics. As you roll the mouse around, the screen image shows a trail that duplicates the movement of the mouse.

The *LogiMouse* instruction manual gives several examples of how the system can be used in business programs like word processors and electronic spreadsheets (for cursor movement), and for creating graphics. *LogiMouse* connects to the computer through the keyboard port. Installation is easy because you unplug the keyboard, plug the *LogiMate* interface in, and connect both the mouse and the keyboard to the *LogiMate* interface. It's an interesting little device.

Mass Storage

One of the most urgent needs of any personal computer user is a method of storing large amounts of information outside the computer. This is important because, without such a device, when the computer is turned off, all your work is lost. It is not practical to spend hours writing a program or doing word processing and then have to start all over the next morning, after you turned off your computer. The family of peripherals that handle this problem are called mass storage systems.

Cassette Recorders

Early models of the IBM PC had cassette storage circuits built in. The regular PC still has them, but they are rarely used. Most people buy at least one disk drive. Cassette storage is slow, often unreliable, and there are few programs available for a cassette-only system.

Disk Drive Systems

A floppy disk is a small, 5½ inch, disk that looks like a 45 RPM phonograph record. It is thin and can bend easily—thus the name floppy disk. These disks are inserted into a disk drive. The disk drive records (saves) or plays (reads) information from the disk in much the same way a cassette drive reads a tape. However, the disk drive can read any part of the disk at any time. The biggest advantage of the disk system is that it saves information from the computer and loads it back into the computer many times faster than a cassette. Programs can be found quickly on a disk. The disk system is also many times more reliable than the cassette system.

Although one drive is far better than no drives at all, you will probably want two. The second drive makes it easier to do things like make a backup copy of an important disk. The IBM PC has space for the disk interface card and two disk drives inside the main case. If you buy all your disk drive accessories from IBM there is only one option: you can get disk drives that store 160K ($289) on a disk or drives that store 320K ($529). We would urge you to pay the extra cost and get the drives that store 320K. These drives are more convenient to use because you can put twice as much on each disk, and they are required for some programs. The 360K drives will work with disks written on systems with 160K drives, so you don't lose compatibility. However, if you select the 160K drive, many business programs that need lots of disk storage won't work on your computer.

You can buy your disk drive system from IBM, but you don't have to. Several companies sell the drives for about half the price of drives from IBM. For example, you can buy 360K disk drives that plug into the IBM PC for between $189 and $250 from at least twenty different companies. You could thus buy the disk interface card from IBM, get your drives from another source, and save several hundred dollars. There are qualitative differences between the various disk drive manufacturers, but if you get drives made by known companies like Tandon, Shugart, Control Data, or MPI, you should get reliable products.

If your mass storage needs are beyond the capacity of ordinary floppy disk drives you can add one or more *hard disk drives* to your system. Hard disks can store from five to fifty million characters. IBM has a ten-megabyte (ten million characters) hard disk drive for the PC, but at least ten other companies sell them. Other companies often sell drives for hundreds, even thousands, of dollars less than the price of equivalent products from IBM. A considerable degree of caution should be exercised while shopping for hard disks for the PC, however. Floppy disk drives from other suppliers are not difficult to integrate into the PC system. Hard disk drives, on the other hand, are not so easy to integrate. Several companies sell hard disk systems for the PC that do not work properly because the operating system software is improperly written or simply has mistakes in the program. If you buy a hard disk drive from anyone other than IBM, we suggest you check out the drive carefully and talk with other PC owners who have used the hard disk long enough to tell you there are no problems with its operation on the PC.

Expansion Cards for the IBM PC

There are at least a hundred different expansion cards currently in production for the IBM PC. Here are brief descriptions of a few of those products:

Microsoft System Card. This product, which is distributed by the company that produced the standard disk operating system for the PC, has several features. It has room for up to 256K of memory, a parallel printer port, and a serial port. It also includes a built-in clock system the computer can use to keep track of the time and data of various transactions.

This card also has the ability to use part of the RAM as a *disk emulator*. That is, the computer can be fooled into thinking the memory on this card is actually a disk drive where material can be stored. Using memory to emulate a disk drive during execution of a program can speed up program operation, particularly in business software where the program receives data from and sends data to the disk frequently. With this card you can use the RAM disk emulator during execution and then transfer data on the disk emulator to a real disk before turning the machine off.

The card can also *spool* data being transmitted to a printer. Spooling lets the computer transmit data to be printed to an intermediate device, which then transfers it to the printer. It takes only a few seconds to transfer data to the spooler circuit. You can then continue using the computer while the spooler takes care of transmitting data to the printer, without waiting for five or ten minutes while the printer does its thing.

Quadram's *Quadlink*. This is a revolutionary card. If you install the *Quadlink* card in the IBM PC, it lets you run virtually all of the programs written for the Apple II computer. You thus have a vast library of game, educational, and business software available to you. When you combine all the software for the IBM PC with all of that for the Apple II, you no doubt have the widest range of quality software available for any computer. This card costs around $680 or less (prices have jumped around a bit since it was announced), but it is a popular card. With this card, you can put an Apple disk in the PC disk drive and run the program as if you had an Apple.

Quadram also sells a very good printer/spooler called the *Microfazer* for computers like the IBM PC. The *Microfazer* accepts as much as 512K of data from the computer in a few seconds and then transmits it to the printer while you continue using the computer. We recommend the *Microfazer* for IBM PC owners who do a lot of printing and don't want to wait while the printer works. Quadram's *Quadboard* for the IBM PC has a parallel port, a serial port, built-in clock with battery backup, and room for up to 256K of memory. Software provided with the board lets you use the memory as a disk drive emulator or as a printer spooler. The *Quadboard* costs $395 with 64K of memory installed.

PC Multipak. This $297 card from Indigo Data Systems gives you four different functions on one card. It has a serial port, a clock with battery backup, and space for up to 256K of RAM. You can add an optional parallel printer port ($30) to the card if you wish. Software that comes with the card lets you use the memory as a disk drive emulator or as memory for a printer spooler.

Also included is software for printing IBM-compatible graphics on an Epson printer and a program that lets you send color graphics to an IDS Prism printer with the optional color printing features.

AST cards. AST Research is a major supplier of accessory cards for the IBM PC. You can buy a wide variety of cards made by AST, including expansion memory, combination cards with serial and parallel ports and memory, cards for connecting game controllers, and specialized cards to interface the PC with larger computers.

Techmar cards. Like AST mentioned above, Techmar pro-

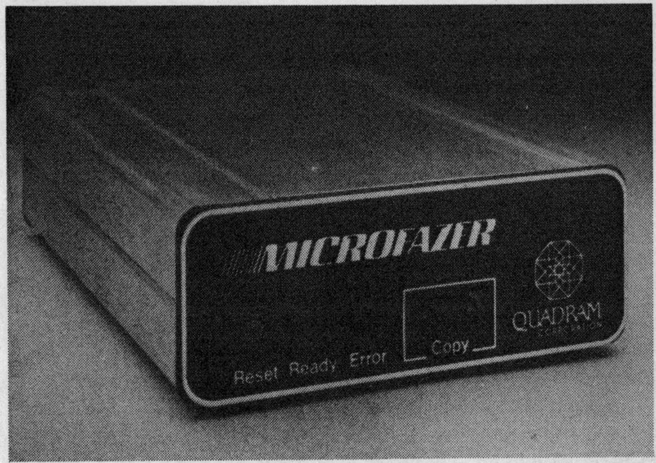

Figure 10.4   Microfazer

duces a wide range of accessories for the PC. In fact, Techmar is probably the best known producer of PC accessories and has one of the best reputations for quality and reliability. The company produces a wider range of products for the PC than any of its competitors.

Monte Carlo card. This five-function card from MBI lets you add from 64K to one million bytes of memory to the computer. It also includes a parallel port, a serial port, a clock with battery backup, and a port for connecting two joysticks. It is a popular card because of the features it combines in one card.

TK ENG card. This card includes room for 256K RAM, a game controller port, and a serial interface. If you are into building your own accessories, you can buy the bare circuit board from TK ENG for $80 and solder the parts on yourself.

This will give you an idea of the type of cards available for the PC. There are hundreds more; we didn't have space to review products from some of the major suppliers such as Apparat, Maynard Electronics, Vista Computer Company, and LNW. You could spend days just looking at all the accessories for the IBM PC.

A CLOSING NOTE ON PERIPHERALS

Whenever you connect a piece of equipment to your computer, you will need some type of connecting cable. These can often be expensive, so make sure they are either included in the cost of the peripheral or that you get a price before you buy the peripheral. Otherwise you may find yourself with a new device you can't use because you can't connect it to your computer. Many standard peripherals will connect to the IBM PC only if you have the expansion box that contains standard serial and parallel I/O ports.

In this brief chapter, we have not covered all the different types of peripherals, much less all the different makes and models. When you set out to add things to your PC, we suggest you do some careful shopping at your local computer store and read some of the magazines written for IBM computer owners.

This concludes *Things To Do With Your IBM Personal Computer*. We hope that you have enjoyed it and that you have learned some useful things. If you haven't bought a computer yet, you might want to read some of the other books in this series. You will find that some of the information in the first part of each chapter is similar to this book. However, the last part of each chapter covers things specific to the computer. One last thing, buying a computer can be either an enjoyable or a frustrating experience. How much you enjoy your computer may depend on how much you find out about it before you buy it. *Happy Computing!*

Glossary

Address: Main memory in a computer is like a grid of thousands of indivual boxes. Each memory location (or box) is called an address.

Alphanumeric: Information presented in both alphabetic and numeric form, for instance a mailing list. The numbers 0–9 and the letters A–Z or any combination.

Applications software: Programs designed to perform specific tasks. Applications software can be games, educational programs, or business programs.

Arithmetic expression: A group of letters, numbers and/or symbols that tell the computer to perform an arithmetic function. For example:

2 + 2

2*2

A22

2/4

2/A

A* (2/B8)

Arithmetic operator: A symbol that tells the computer to perform — subtraction; * multiplication; / division; and ^ raise to a power.

ASCII: A simple code system that converts symbols and numbers into numbers the computer can understand. For instance, when you type *a* on the keyboard of your computer, the binary number 01100001 is sent to computer's central processing unit (CPU). The CPU then displays the letter *a* on the screen.

Assembly language: A low-level programming language that is much faster than a high-level language such as BASIC. Assembly language programs are extremely difficult to write. Here are two lines from an assembly language program:
LDA
MOV C,A

BASIC: Beginner's All-purpose Symbolic Instruction Code. A high-level computer language designed for beginners. Here are four lines of a program written in BASIC:
10 PRINT "HELLO HOW ARE YOU?"
20 DIM A$ (10)
30 INPUT A$
40 GOSUB 500

Baud: A unit of information transfer. In microcomputers, a baud is one bit per second.

Baud rate: The rate at which information is transferred. For instance, 300 baud is a transfer rate of 300 bits per second. This means that each character, space, or symbol requires eight bits. Therefore, a baud rate of 300 transfers only 37.5 characters per second. If you are sending a letter with each word approximately six characters long and you have one space between words, you can send about five words a second or 300 words a minute.

Binary number: A number system that uses only two digits, 0 and 1, to express all numeric values. See digital computer.

Bit: The basic unit of computer memory. It is short for binary digit and can have a value of either 1 or 0.

Black box: A piece of equipment that is viewed only in terms of its input and output.

Boot: The process of loading part or all of the disk operating system into the computer. This lets you load information from the disk or save information to the disk.

Break: To interrupt execution of a program.

Buffer: A temporary storage place used to hold data for further processing.

Bug: A problem that causes the computer or a computer program to perform incorrectly or not at all.

Bus: A set of connection lines between various components of the computer.

Byte: A group of eight bits usually treated as a unit. It takes one byte to store a unit of information. For instance the word *love* requires four bytes.

CAI: Computer-Aided Instruction.

Canned software: One or more programs that are ready to run "as is."

Cartridge: a $2 \times 3 \times \frac{3}{4}$-inch plastic box that contains ROM software such as BASIC.

Cassette: A small plastic cartridge that has magnetic tape inside. It has two reels. The tape on one reel is wound onto the other reel. Computer programs can be stored on a standard audio cassette.

Cassette drive: A standard tape recorder used to save (record) or load (retrieve) computer information.

Cathode ray tube (CRT): The picture tube of a television set or monitor. It is used to display computer output.

Central processing unit (CPU): This is the heart of the computer. It contains the circuits that control the execution of instructions.

Chip: A formed flake of silicon or other semiconductor material containing an integrated circuit.

Circuit: The complete path of an electric current. A computer circuit may have thousands of different elements, i.e., transistors, diodes, resistors, etc.

Circuit board: A plastic board that has hundreds or even thousands of different circuits.

Clock: An electronic circuit in a computer that is the source of timing and synchronizing signals.

Code: A system of symbols and rules for representing, transmitting, and storing information.

Coding: Writing a computer program.

Command: An instruction that tells the computer to perform an operation immediately. The command *RUN*, for instance, tells the computer to begin immediately executing a program.

Compiler: A computer program that translates high-level language statements into machine language.

Computer-aided instruction: The process of teaching by computer. This is a system of individualized instruction that uses a computer program as the learning medium.

Console: The keyboard and other devices that make up the control unit of a computer.

Control key: Pushing the computer's control key in conjunction with another key causes the computer to perform special functions.

Controller: A device that can be attached directly to the computer or to an external mechanical device so that images on the screen can be moved around. A joystick is a controller.

CP/M: An operating system that runs on many different computers.

CPU: Central processing unit.

CRT: Cathode ray tube.

Cursor: The little flashing white square on the CRT that indicates where the next character will be displayed.

Daisy wheel printer: A printing maching whose print head has a number (usually 96) of radial arms or petals. Each petal has a type character on the end. Daisy wheel type is equal to or better than most typewriter type.

Data: All items of information a computer can process or generate—numbers, letters, symbols, facts, statements, etc.

Database: The entire collection of data in a computer system that can be accessed at one time.

Database management system: A program that organizes data in a computer's data storage so that several, or all, programs can have access to virtually any item, and yet a particular item need be keyed into the computer system only once.

Data processing: The process of converting data into machine readable form so the computer can work on it.

Data transmission rate: Baud rate.

Debug: To eliminate errors in a computer or a computer program.

Decimal number system: This is the number system you are familiar with, that is, 0–9.

Default: See default value.

Default value: An assigned quantity for a device or program that is set by the manufacturer. For instance, a printer may have a default value that tells it to print everything in elite type. A default value in a program is usually the most common or safest answer. As another example, a word processing program may ask if you want to clear everything in memory. The safest answer is no, since it doesn't cause any harm if you hit the wrong key. In this example the program would have a default value of no.

Desktop computer: A complete computer system designed to fit on a desktop.

Device: Any piece of computer equipment.

Digital: A system that uses the number 0 and 1 to represent variables involved in calculation. This means that information can be represented by a series of offs (0) or ons (1). See bit.

Digital computer: A computer that uses a series of electronic offs and ons to represent information. These offs and ons are converted to (or from) binary numbers. The IBM is a digital computer.

Directory: A list of all the files on a diskette.

Disc: Disk

Disk: A piece of flat rotating circular mylar that is coated with magnetic material. It is used to store computer information. See also hard disk and diskette.

Diskette: A flexible disk that is 5¼ inches in diameter (about the size of a 45 RPM record). It is the most common mass storage device.

Disk drive: An electromechanical device that stores on or recalls information from a disk.

Disk file: An organized collection of data stored on a disk.

Disk operating system: An operating system that let's a computer use one or more disk drives. See operating system.

Documentation: All of the available information about a particular computer, computer program, or set of programs; it would include instructions on how to turn on the computer, how to load programs, and so on. For computer programs, the documentation should include such information as what type of computer the program runs on, how much memory is needed, and how to operate the program. The Texas Instruments CC-40 comes with an owner's manual.

DOS: Disk operating system.

Dot matrix printer: A printer that forms characters as patterns of dots. The dots lie within a grid of definite dimensions, such as 5×7 dots.

Dual density: A technique of writing twice as much information on a diskette.

Edit: To make changes on the screen in data or a program.

Electronic mail: Personal or other messages generated on computer and transmitted to another computer at a different location. The computers are connected by phone lines.

Execute: To operate a computer program or part of a computer program. The process a computer goes through when it analyzes instructions and acts on them.

Expression: A combination of numbers, variables, and operators that can be evaluated. The answer must be a single number or variable. For instance, $2 + 3 = 5$. It can't equal 7. Other expressions such as $A + B$, $A - 3$ or $A/B*38$ must also have only one answer.

External memory: Mass storage.

Field: A unit of information that is part of a file. For instance, in the following mailing list file, NAME, ADDRESS, CITY, STATE, and ZIP are all fields:

NAME________________

ADDRESS________________

CITY________________

STATE________

ZIP________

In the example above, both the information and title are part of a field. For instance, the field for Joe Jones is this: NAME Joe Jones.

File: An organized collection of related records. A payroll file has a complete payroll record for each employee.

Floppy disk: Diskette.

Formatting: The process of electronically organizing a diskette so that information can be stored on it and retrieved from it.

FORTRAN: FORmula TRANslation. A high-level computer language used for mathematical or engineering applications. Here are three lines from a FORTRAN program:

40 FORMAT (E14.7)

X = A + B*C/D − E

WRITE (6, 50)X

Function key: A key that tells the computer to perform a special function. These functions are defined by the programmer.

Graphics: Pictures, line drawings, and special characters that can be displayed on the screen or produced by a printer.

Hard copy: A copy of the computer's output printed on paper.

Hard disk: A mass storage device that uses a rotating rigid disk made of a hard plastic-like material. It has many times the storage capacity of a diskette.

Hardware: The various physical components of a computer system, such as the computer itself, the printer, keyboard, and monitor.

High-level language: A computer language that uses simple English words to represent computer commands. For instance, the command PRINT "Hello" in BASIC tells the computer to print the word *Hello* on the screen.

Initialize: To set a program element or hardware device to an initial quantity (usually zero).

Input: To transfer data from the keyboard or a mass storage device into the computer's internal memory.

Input device: A device used to enter information into a computer. These are all input devices: keyboard, joystick, disk drive, cassette player.

Input-Output: The processing of entering data into a computer or taking it out.

Integrated circuit: A group of components that form a complete miniaturized electronic circuit. The circuit has a number of transistors plus associated circuits. These components are fabricated together on a single piece of semiconductor material.

Interactive: A computer system that responds immediately to user input.

Interface: A device that allows other devices to communicate with each other; a modem, for instance.

Inverse video: A process that shows dark text on a light background on your screen. Normally light text is shown on a dark background.

I/O: Input/Output.

Jack: A plug socket on a computer.

Joystick controller: A two-inch by two-inch black box with a movable plastic stick on the top of it. It is used as an input device most often with computer games.

K: When used as a measure of computer memory K is an abbreviation for kilobyte or kilobytes. It is also an abbreviation for kilo.

Kilo: A prefix meaning 1000. In computer jargon it is used as an abbreviation for 1024.

Kilobyte: 1024 bytes. Thus 4 kilobytes (abbreviated 4K) of memory is about 4000 bytes of memory. It is exactly 4096 bytes, but 4K is a convenient way to keep track of it. This means that if you have 4K of memory, you have space for 4096 characters, spaces, numbers, and symbols in your computer.

Language: The means of communicating. The difference between computer language and human language is that a computer language allows humans to communicate with computers. The lowest level of language is machine language; the *pure* language of the computer. Machine language programs use 1's and 0's to represent the on's and off's in the computer. Machine language programs are the most difficult programs to write but they do not have the speed and action limitations of higher level languages. Assembly language programs are also low-level languages but they use simple mnemonic statements as commands. High-level languages such as BASIC, FORTRAN, and Logo, use English-like statements to tell the computer what to do. BASIC is the most common language because it is the simplest to use.

Load: The process of entering data or programs from an external device, such as a disk drive, into the computer. For instance, if you *load* a program into the computer it is available for use.

Line number: A number that defines each line of programming in a high-level language. Each line of the program begins with a line number. The computer executes the program in line number order starting with the lowest number.

Logic: A systematized interconnection of devices in a computer circuit that cause it to perform certain functions.

Logical operator: A symbol that tells the computer to make a comparison. These operators include $>$ (greater than), $<$ (less than), and $=$ (equals).

Logo: A high-level computer language that is often used by children. An easy to learn language, Logo allows colorful, detailed graphics to be drawn on the screen. Sprite graphics and turtle graphics are terms associated with Logo.

Loop: A series of programming instructions that repeat. The last instruction in the loop tells the computer to return to the first instruction. Intentional loops have some means of escape built into them. Unintentional loops, caused by programmer error, can only be stopped by pressing the escape key or turning the computer off.

Low-level language: A computer language at the machine level (a pattern of pure binary coding). It is neither simple nor obvious for a human being to read, understand, or use.

Machine language: The lowest-level language. It is a pattern of ones and zeros that the computer understands.

Mail merging: A program usually used with word processing that allows you to insert names and addresses into a group of documents. All you have to do is load the names and a sample of the document; everything else is automatic. For instance, suppose you want to send the same letter to 2000 people. Once you have created the mail list and the letter, the computer adds the name and address of the first person to an original copy of the letter. It can also address the person by name at several different places in the letter. It does the same thing for the second person on the list, the third, and so on.

Mainframe computer: A large expensive computer generally used for data processing in large corporations and government installations. Originally, the term referred to the extensive array of large rack and panel cabinets that held thousands of vacuum tubes in the early computers.

Mass storage: The files of computer data that are stored on media other than the computer's memory. For example, diskettes and cassettes are mass storage devices.

Matrix printer: Dot matrix printer

Mega: A prefix meaning one million.

Memory: The internal hardware in the computer that stores information for further use.

Menu: A display shown on the screen that gives you a list of options. You select an option by typing a letter or number and pressing the return key.

Microcomputer: A fully operational computer that uses a microprocessor as its CPU. Microcomputers are a new kind of computer. Whereas minicomputers are small-scale versions of large computers, microcomputers are an outgrowth of semiconductor technology. Consequently, some microcomputers have features not found on either minicomputers or mainframe computers.

Microprocessor: A central processing unit contained on a single silicon chip.

Minidisk: Diskette.

Minicomputer: A small computer based on large computer technology.

Mnemonic: A technique or symbol designed to aid the human memory. Its most common computer use is in assembly language programming. For instance, it is much easier to remember LDA (an assembly language term) than 004000 072.

Mnemonic code: A system of abbreviations designed to replace obscure, complex terms used in preparing assembly language programs.

Modeling: A partial simulation of real or possible situations.

Modem: A modulating and demodulating device that enables computers to communicate over telephone lines.

Monitor: A television or cathode ray tube used to display computer information. In common usage, a monitor usually refers to a special device used exclusively for computer output. It can display a line 80 characters long and has at least 24 lines of text.

Mylar: A type of plastic used in the manufacture of floppy disks.

Nano: One billionth.

Nanosecond: One billionth of a second. Modern computers operate in nanoseconds.

Numeric data: Data that consists entirely of numbers.

Operating system: A set of computer programs devoted to the operation of the computer itself. The operating system must be present in the computer before applications programs can be loaded or run.

OS: Operating system.

Output: Information or data transferred from the internal memory of the computer to some external device.

Output device: A device used to take information out of a computer. CRTs, mass storage devices (such as disk drives), and printers are all output devices.

Packaged software: Canned software.

Parallel: The performance of two or more operations or functions simultaneously. For instance, a parallel port accepts all eight bits of a byte at one time. Some printers are connected to the computer via the parallel port.

Pascal: A powerful high-level computer language for business and general use. Named for French mathematician and philosopher Blaise Pascal (1623–1662). Here are three lines from a Pascal program:

```
BEGIN
READLN (I,HOURS)
IF I = 1 THEN WORK: = SUN
```

PC: Personal computer.

Peripheral: Any device that connects to a computer. Printers, joysticks, and modems are peripherals.

Personal computer: Microcomputer.

PILOT: This is an easy-to-learn, high-level language designed for novice computer users. Primarily used for educational programs.

Pixel: A picture element that is one point on a screen. The size of the pixel depends on the computer graphics mode being used and the resolution capabilities of the screen.

Port: The location where Input/Output devices are connected to the computer. For example, a printer may be connected to the computer with a cable at the parallel port. A modem may be connected at the serial port.

Power supply: A device, consisting of a transformer and other components, that converts household current (115 or 220 volt) to the voltage used by a computer.

Printer: A device for producing paper copies (hard copy) of the data output by a computer.

Program: An organized group of instructions that tells the computer what to do. The program must be in a language the computer understands.

Prompt: A symbol, usually a question mark, appearing on the screen that asks you to enter information.

QWERTY: An abbreviation used to indicate a standard typewriter-style keyboard. The first six letters in the third row of a standard keyboard are QWERTY.

RAM: Random Access Memory.

Random Access Memory: This is the read-write memory available for use in the computer. Through random access the computer can retrieve or send information instantly at any memory address. See memory.

Read: The act of taking data from a storage device, such as a diskette, and putting it in the computer's memory.

Read Only Memory: A random access memory device that contains permanently stored information. The contents of this memory are set during manufacture. A game cartridge is a Read Only Memory.

Read/Write memory: Computer memory that you can put data into or take data out of at any time.

Record: An organized block of data. For instance, the payroll information on one person.

Resolution: The number of points (or pixels) you can put on a television screen (or monitor) both vertically and horizontally. High resolution indicates a large number of pixels and, therefore, a sharper display.

Reverse video: Inverse video.

ROM: Read Only Memory.

SAVE: A command that tells the computer to store the contents of memory on some media, such as a diskette or cassette.

Screen: A CRT or television screen.

Semiconductor: A metal or other material (silicon, for example) with properties between those of conductors and insulators. Its electrical resistance can be changed by electricity, light, or heat.

Serial: A group of events that happen one at a time in sequence. For instance, a serial interface reads in a byte one bit at a time. Modems transmit data serially.

Silicon: A nonmetallic chemical element resembling carbon. It is used in the manufacture of transistors, solar cells, etc.

Software: The programs and data used to control a computer. Software is available in many forms. You can type the program in yourself or you can have it transmitted to you over the telephone. You can also get it on cassette, diskette, or cartridge.

System: All of the various hardware components that make the computer usable, such as the computer, printer, modem, keyboard, CRT, and disk drive or cassette player.

Text editor: A computer program that allows you to change or modify the contents of memory. It can modify either data or programs.

Turtle graphics: A small, triangular shape that is displayed on the screen when the language Logo is used. The *turtle* shows the direction of lines for graphics. For example, if the instruction is to move north, then the turtle moves toward the top of the screen.

User-friendly: A computer system or software package that is easy for novice users to use and understand.

User's-manual: A book or notebook that describes how to use a particular piece of equipment or software.

Variable: A quantity that can assume any of a given set of values. For instance, assume A is a variable whose value is 1. If you add 3 to it, its value becomes 4.

Video display: The screen of your monitor or TV.

Volatile memory: As used with computers, volatile means that the memory loses its contents when the computer is turned off. That is, any information in volatile memory is lost when the computer is turned off.

Window: A portion of the CRT display devoted to a specific purpose.

Word: A minimum storage element in computer memory and the smallest data element worked on by the CPU. Word sizes vary with the design of the computer, varying from eight bits to 12, 16, 32, or 64 bits.

Word processing: A special feature of a computer that allows you to manipulate text. See also word processor or text editor.

Word processor: A computer program that helps you manipulate text. You can write a document, insert or change words, paragraphs or pages, and then print the document letter-perfect.

Write: To store data on external media such as a disk or cassette. The expression *write to diskette* means that the information stored in the computer's memory is sent to the diskette where it is stored.

Write protect: When new material is written to a diskette, any old material there is erased. Write protect is a method of fixing the disk so that it can't be written on.

Software Publishers

Abacus Associates
6565 W. Loop South
Suite #240
Bellaire, Texas 77401
(713) 666-8164

Advanced Operating Systems
450 St. John Road
Michigan City, Indiana 46360
(800) 348-8558

Alpha Software Corporation
12 New England Executive
  Park
Burlington, Massachusetts
  01803
(617) 229-2924

Artificial Intelligence
  Research Group
921 North La Jolla Avenue
Los Angeles, California 90046
(213) 654-2214
(213) 656-7368

Ashton Tate
10150 W. Jefferson Blvd.
Culver City, California 90230
(213) 204-5570

Aspen Software Co.
P.O. Box 339
Tijeras, New Mexico 87059
(505) 281-3371

Automated Simulations
P.O. Box 4247
Mountain View, California
  94040
(408) 745-0700

Avalon Hill
4517 Harford Rd.
Baltimore, Maryland 21214
(800) 638-9292

Avant-Garde Creations, Inc.
P.O. Box 30160
Eugene, Oregon 97403
(503) 345-3043

Blue Chip Software
19824 Ventura Blvd., #125
Woodland Hills, California
  91364
(213) 881-8288

BV Engineering
P.O. Box 3351
Riverside, California 92519
(714) 781-0252

Byte
McGraw-Hill, Inc.
70 Main St.
Peterborough, New Hampshire 03458
(603) 924-9281

Cdex Corporation
5050 El Camino Real
Suite 200
Los Altos, California 94022
(415) 964-7600

Comprehensive Software
  Support
2316 Artesia Blvd.
Suite B
Redondo Beach, California
  90278
(213) 318-2561

CompuServe
5000 Arlington Centre Boulevard
Columbus, Ohio 43220
(614) 457-8600 Headquarters
(614) 224-3113 Branch Office

Computer in the School:
  Tutor, Tool, Tutee, The
Columbia University Press
562 W. 113 St.
New York, New York 10025
(212) 316-7100

Computer Music Journal, The
MIT Press Journals
28 Carlton St.
Cambridge, Massachusetts
  02142
(617) 253-2889

Computers in the Schools
Haworth Press
28 E. 22 St.
New York, New York 10010
(212) 228-2800

Computer Sports Systems
22458 Ventura Blvd.
Suite E
Woodland Hills, California
  91364
(213) 992-0514

Computing Teacher, The
Computing Center
Eastern Oregon State College
La Grande, Oregon 97850
(503) 963-1582

Compuview Products, Inc.
1955 Pauline Blvd.
Suite 200
Ann Arbor, Michigan 48103
(313) 996-1299

Continental Software
11223 South Hindry Ave.
Los Angeles, California 90045
(213) 417-8031
(213) 417-3003

Datamension Corporation
615 Academy Drive
Northbrook, Illinois 60062
(312) 564-5060

DesignWare
185 Berry St.
San Francisco, California
   94107
(800) 572-7767

Digital Research, Inc.
P.O. Box 597
160 Central Avenue
Pacific Grove, California
   93950

Distributed Computing
   Systems
P.O. Box 185
Lombard, Illinois 60148
(312) 495-0121

Distributed Software Sys-
   tems, Inc.
P.O. Box 1301
Northbrook, Illinois 60062
(312) 634-1511

DLM, Inc. (Developmental
   Learning Materials)
One DLM Park
P.O. Box 4000
Allen, Texas 75002
(214) 248-6300

Don't Ask Computer Soft-
   ware
2265 Westwood Boulevard
Suite B-150
Los Angeles, California 90064
(213) 477-4514
(213) 397-8811

*Educational Computer Mag-
   azine*
P.O. Box 535
Cupertino, California 95015
(408) 252-3224

Ensign Software
2312 N. Cole Rd.
Suite E
Boise, Idaho 83704
(208) 378-8086

Epyx
1043 Kiel Court
Sunnyvale, California 94089
(408) 745-0700

Europro, Inc.
129 Saratoga
Petaluma, California 94952
(707) 763-9700

Friendly Soft, Inc.
3609 Smith-Barry Rd.
Arlington, Texas 76013
(817) 277-9378

Hexagon Systems
P.O. Box 397
Station A
Vancouver B.C., Canada
   V6C 2N2
(604) 682-7646

Howard Software Services
8008 Girard Avenue
Suite 310
La Jolla, California
   92037
(619) 454-0121

IBM Systems Products Division
P.O. Box 1328
Boca Raton, Florida 33432
(305) 241-7662
(305) 241-7006

Infocom, Inc.
55 Wheeler Street
Cambridge, Massachusetts
   02138
(617) 492-1031

InfoWorld Magazine
530 Lytton
Palo Alto, California 94301
(415) 328-4602

Insoft
P.O. Box 19208
Portland, Oregon 97219
(503) 641-5223

Interface Age
McPheters, Wolfe, & Jones
16704 Marguardt Avenue
Cerritos, California 90701

Krell Software Corporation
1320 Stony Brook Road
Stony Brook, New York
   11790
(516) 751-5139

Laboratory Microsystems
4147 Beethoven Street
Los Angeles, California 90066
(213) 306-7412

Lexisoft, Inc
P.O. Box 1378
Davis, California 95617
(916) 758-3630

Lifeboat Associates
1651 Third Avenue
New York, New York 10028
(212) 860-0300

Lightning Software, Inc.
P.O. Box 11725
Palo Alto, California 94306
(415) 327-3280

Lotus Development Corp.
161 First St.
Cambridge, Massachusetts
   02142
(617) 492-7171

Mark of the Unicorn, Inc.
P.O. Box 423
Arlington, Massachusetts
 02174
(617) 576-2760

Masterworks Software, Inc.
25834 Narbonne Ave.
Lomita, California 90717
(213) 539-7486

Metamorphics, Inc.
154 Montgomery Ave.
Bala Cynwood, Pennsylvania
 19004
(215) 668-9000

Micro Architect, Inc.
#6 Great Pine Ave.
Burlington, Massachusetts
 01803
(617) 273-5658

Micro Data Base Systems,
 Inc.
P.O. Box 248
Lafayette, Indiana 47902
(317) 463-2581

MicroPro International Corp.
33 San Pablo Ave.
San Rafael, California 94903
(415) 499-1200
(800) 227-2400

Microsoft Corporation
10700 Northrup Way
Suite 200
Bellevue, Washington 98004
(206) 828-8088

Micro-Systems Software, Inc.
4301-18 Oak Circle
Boca Raton, Florida 33431
(305) 983-3390

Mindstorms
Harper & Row Publishers,
 Inc.
10 E. 53 St.
New York, New York 10022
(212) 207-7000

Mirror Images Software, Inc.
1223 Peoples Ave.
Troy, New York 12180
(518) 274-2335

New Venture Systems
P.O. Box 2141
Chesapeake, Virginia 23320
(804) 482-1889

NODVILL Software
24 Nod Road
Ridgefield, Connecticut 06877
(203) 431-6449

Norell Data Systems
3400 Wilshire Blvd.
P.O. Box 70127
Los Angeles, California 90010
(213) 257-2026

Omniware
8972 East Hampden Ave.
P.O. Box 32
Denver, Colorado 80231

Padware Limited
P.O. Box 14856
Chicago, Illinois 60614
(312) 248-5004

PBL Corporation
P.O. Box 559
Wayzata, Minnesota 55391
(612) 473-8998

PC Magazine
P.O. Box 2445
Boulder, Colorado 80321

PC Software
4155 Cleveland Ave.
San Diego, California 92103

PC World
PC World Communications,
   Inc.
555 De Haro St.
San Francisco, California
   94107
(415) 861-3861

Persoft, Inc.
2740 Ski Lane
Madison, Wisconsin 53713
(608) 233-1000

Personal Computing
Hayden Publishing Co., Inc.
50 Essex St.
Rochelle Park, New Jersey
   07662

Popular Computing
McGraw-Hill, Inc.
70 Main St.
Peterborough, New Hamp-
   shire 03458
(603) 924-9281

Proximity Devices Corp.
3511 NE 22nd Ave.
Fort Lauderdale, Florida
   33308
(800) 323-0023
(305) 566-3511

Quinsept, Inc.
P.O. Box 216
Lexington,   Massachusetts
   02173
(617) 862-0404

QSI Software
P.O. Box 3–231 ECB
Anchorage, Alaska 99501
(907) 265-8187

Sirius Software, Inc.
10364 Rockingham Dr.
Sacramento, California 95827
(916) 366-1195

Softalk
Softalk Publishing, Inc.
11160 McCormick St.
North Hollywood, California
    91601
(213) 980-5074

Software Laboratories, Inc.
6924 Riverside Dr.
Dublin, Ohio 43017
(800) 531-1309

Software Options, Inc.
19 Rector St.
New York, New York 10006
(212) 785-8285

Software Solutions, Inc.
305 Bic Drive
Milford, Connecticut 06460
(203) 877-9268

Solutions, Inc.
Box 989
Montpelier, Vermont 05602
(802) 229-0368

Sorcim
2310 Lundy Ave.
San Jose, California 95131
(408) 942-1727

Source Telecomputing
    Corporation
1616 Anderson Road
McLean, Virginia 22102
(703) 821-6660

Spinnaker Software
215 First St.
Cambridge, Massachusetts
    02142
(617) 868-4700

Sunburst Communications
Room MM
39 Washington Ave.
Pleasantville, New York
    10570
(800) 431-1934

Supersoft, Inc.
P.O. Box 1628
Champaign, Illinois 61820
(217) 359-2112

Systemics, Inc.
3050 Spring St.
West Bloomfield, Michigan
    48033
(313) 851-2504

TCI Software
6107 West Mill Road
Flourtown, Pennsylvania
    19031
(215) 836-1406

User-Friendly Software, Inc.
P.O. Box 1192
Melville, New York 11747
(516) 643-6618

Virtual Combinatics
Box 755
Rockport, Massachusetts
    01966
(617) 546-6553

VisiCorp
2895 Zanker Rd.
San Jose, California 95134
(408) 946-9000

VORTRAX
500 Stephenson Hwy.
Troy, Michigan 48048
(800) 521-1350
(313) 588-2050

Zork User's Group
Dept. Z0
P.O. Box 20923
Milwaukee, Wisconsin 53220

Index

All About Computers from SIGNET and SIGNET DILITHIUM

(0451)

☐ **COMPUTERS FOR EVERYBODY by Jerry Willis and Merl Miller.** The comprehensive, up-to-date, easy-to-understand guide that answers the question: What can a personal computer do for you? Whatever your needs and interests, this book can help you find the personal computer that will fill the bill. (128400—$3.50)*

☐ **BITS, BYTES AND BUZZWORDS: Understanding Small Business Computers by Mark Garetz.** If you run a small business, the time has come for you to find out what a computer is, what it does, and what it can do for you. With expert authority, and in easy-to-understand language, this essential handbook takes the mystery and perplexity out of computerese and tells you all you need to know. (128419—$2.95)*

☐ **EASY-TO-UNDERSTAND GUIDE TO HOME COMPUTERS by the Editors of** *Consumer Guide*. This handbook cuts through the tech-talk to tell you clearly—in Plain English—exactly what computers are, how they work, and why they're so amazingly useful. Includes information needed to understand computing, to use computer equipment and programs and even do your own programming. A special buying section compares the most popular home computers on the market. (120310—$3.95)*

☐ **KEN USTON'S GUIDE TO HOME COMPUTERS by Ken Uston.** In language you can understand—the most accessible and up-to-date guide you need to pick the personal computer that's best for you! Leading video game and home computer expert Ken Uston takes the mystery out of personal computers as he surveys the ever-growing, often confusing home computer market. (125975—$3.50)

*Prices slightly higher in Canada
